AN
OUT OF BODY LIFE

*A GUIDE TO ENDING SUFFERING
ONCE AND FOR ALL*

Bradley L. Morris II

HARPU COLLECTIVE

ISBN (Paperback): 979-8-9931423-0-2
ISBN (Hardback): 979-8-9931423-1-9

Printed in the United States of America

To the One

CONTENTS

Introduction

INTRODUCTION

THE SECRET OF THE UNIVERSE: YOU

Most great teachers and thought leaders would recommend that I take you, the reader, through a journey, a step-by-step process from step one to step two and so forth until we arrive at the conclusion. The idea is to provide something for everyone as we turn the pages, to gradually butter you up before revealing the secrets of the Universe. But that is not what I intend to do in this book. Instead, I will begin with the conclusion, and then I will unravel it in such a way that you can embody it all and completely transform the way you experience existence itself.

Most Wisdom Traditions around the world require decades of practice before you can finally reach enlightenment. Even then, most of those traditions teach that true enlightenment can only be achieved after death. The good news about what I am going to teach you is that you can be fully enlightened by the end of this book. It is achievable for everyone right now, whether you come from a spiritual or religious background or if you are a total atheist. The requirement is not faith, it is not belief, and it is not wisdom – it is simply Insight.

Historically, a meaningful debate would only begin when each participant could clearly articulate the opposing viewpoint. Therefore, I will begin this section by reciting the two leading ideas for the origin and nature of consciousness, or rather, the origin of all things.

The first theory of the origin of the Universe is materialism. The second theory is idealism, or spiritualism. I will propose a third idea that transcends both leading age theories of human consciousness, and the study of all that is. In the third idea, we will use ontology (a metaphysical approach to defining "what is") and epistemology (a philosophical approach to defining "how we know"), along with other tools, as a basis for constructing a framework for thought.

Today, we fallaciously separate science and spirituality, but in ancient days, the sage was both a scientist and a religious leader. This book rekindles the relationship between science and spirituality and, in fact, shows that at the core of all science and religion, we are simply saying the same thing from different perspectives. The third idea, which is the key to living

An Out of Body Life, explains the deep gaps in leading consciousness and metaphysical theories, as well as in the leading wisdom traditions, which cease to exist when the two lie on top of one another.

The philosophy of materialism suggests that all things come from matter only. Matter is the fundamental reality, and all phenomena simply result from brain activities and/or material reactions in space and time. Consequently, from a materialist perspective, consciousness is understood to be a phenomenon emerging from matter.

The belief in spiritualism (also called idealism) is the opposite. According to spiritualist perspectives, consciousness is considered primary, with matter, time, and space subsequently originating from or manifesting within it. In other words, to make it easily digestible to everyone, the term consciousness could also be called Spirit. Of course, the conservative materialist doesn't believe that there is a spirit, and the conservative spiritualist would use the word spirit (or God) instead of consciousness to describe the creator of the universe. These are merely semantics, and this book rips the semantics to shreds to establish a clear picture.

From the materialist's point of view, matter is the fundamental and only substance in the world we perceive today. Materialists argue that human consciousness is simply the byproduct of complex brain patterns and that all psychological phenomena (emotions, intellect, thinking, etc.)

can be traced back to specific parts of the brain. The materialist affirms that there is no spiritual realm, and everything that has ever existed or will exist is nothing more than a series of atomic and subatomic reactions, largely random in nature.

Explaining complex ideas by breaking them down to the level of quarks and superstrings (in some metaphysical interpretations of human consciousness) is called reductionism. Philosopher David Chalmers articulated a concept that, for now, seriously challenges materialism, which is called "the hard problem of consciousness." Even though scientists can map out every neural firing into various chemical reactions that explain most human experiences, the hard problem of consciousness is that it is impossible to explain how brain activity produces subjective experiences. Materialism can describe how the brain processes information and controls behavior, or even integrates sensory data, but not how or why humans feel what they feel. In simple terms, we know that brain activity causes pain, but brain activity cannot explain what pain feels like to humans. This means that there is likely something subtler than the matter alone, which is the *experiencer* of the experienced.

The spiritualist will argue that matter is not the fundamental (and certainly not the only) substance we perceive in the world today. The spiritualist argues that there was first consciousness (some spiritualists call this "God"), and then, out of consciousness, came all matter we see around us.

Spiritualists agree that the Big Bang could have happened, but even if it did, it was God who set it in motion.

In 2016, Galen Strawson suggested in the New York Times that there is no hard problem of consciousness; he wrote, "consciousness isn't a mystery. It's matter." He contends that matter is actually the problem, so he coined the term "hard problem of matter." Consciousness is not mysterious because we all experience it every waking (and sleeping) moment of our lives. We know what pain feels like, what heartbreak entails, joy, hearing, etc. What we can't explain are physical things.

In modern psychology, there is a concept known as mindfulness, and one of its key practices is body scanning. To participate in a body scan, we slowly imagine every part of our body from our toes up to our head. In doing so, we become mindful of the present moment and deeply connected to our physical being, often experiencing peace and a feeling of awakening. Yet this raises an intriguing question: Why are all humans PhDs at body scans and can vividly describe the subjective feelings inside our individual selves, but most of us have no clue how to explain physical phenomena like gravity, the weather, or the nature of a light photon? And why is it that actual PhDs in the material world can't explain Black Holes, the origin of the Universe, or any other complex material realities? This seems to mean that consciousness is fundamental, and matter was created from consciousness.

To take this a step further and to confuse experiencers all around the world a little more, some spiritualists believe that the purpose of existence (because there must be a purpose, right?) is for the conscious to learn and understand all the material things it created. Like a quarterback that throws the ball to a wide receiver, the experience we call life is simply humans running to catch the ball that the quarterback, called God, threw. Eventually, humans naturally began to measure how well they played this game of life, labeling experiences as good or bad, success or failure, and then we started defining ourselves by our performance in the game of life.

To make the eternal linear and feel a sense of satisfaction, humans pondered the idea of spiritual growth through past lives and future lives. They believe that there is something to be achieved, and if we do not achieve it in this lifetime, we will achieve it in the next. They strive for spiritual perfection so that they can achieve Nirvana once and for all.

Other spiritualists, like most Christians, believe in only one life and then one afterlife. Though, if you really get deep into their philosophies, you will see that deeply embedded in their doctrines is the idea of multiple lifetimes – for example, Christian theologians believe in Christophanies, where Jesus was incarnated multiple times in the Old and New Testament (as the "dabar" of the Lord, possibly Melchizedek, definitely the Angel of the Lord that sat with Abraham in Genesis 18 and also in Judges 6 to Gideon and Joshua 5 to Joshua, among other times). He also experienced a "life" in the New Testament and then entered another body after death (as commonly explained in mainstream Christianity). Elijah, Moses, and many other Bible characters also lived in multiple bodies in the Abrahamic scriptures, though followers of the mainstream religions often reject the idea of multiple incarnations.

Across these belief systems, the common theme is that there is a "right" way and a "wrong" way to do this complex experience we call life, and that there is a heaven and a hell that can either be experienced while living (Jivanmukta or Moksha in Indian philosophies) or after death (Heaven in the Bible). But all these traditions are only somewhat true. Numerous hybrids of idealistic and materialistic theories exist, which I will not detail here since other works cover them thoroughly (google "325 theories of consciousness" by Robert Kuhn, if you would like to get lost in that rabbit hole). They all have small holes in them that are filled when they interact with each other.

So, are you ready for the secret to the great mystery of this existence? Great, well here it is.

Not only do you have past lives and future lives, but you have lived this exact life an infinite number of times, doing it a little differently each time. You've written this book as me, and I have read this book as you, there is no difference between us, for there is only one fundamental reality, and it is experiencing itself. We call this reality God, Spirit, consciousness, and many other things, but these are merely words that we invented which are describing the same truth. This is enlightenment.

You can stop reading this book altogether now and just meditate on this truth for the rest of your life. You will not be enlightened, but you will certainly have more peace knowing that you can't really get anything wrong because you have an infinite number of "tries" to get it right. But

"NOT ONLY DO YOU HAVE PAST LIVES AND FUTURE LIVES, BUT YOU HAVE LIVED THIS EXACT LIFE AN INFINITE NUMBER OF TIMES, DOING IT A LITTLE DIFFERENTLY EACH TIME"

if you would like a full breakthrough, keep reading.

Before we proceed, let me welcome you home again. I, as the writer this time around, am elated to share the Wisdom with you, and I am thankful for the many times you shared it with me. This is not the first time you have received this Gospel, the very fact that you are reading this book now means that you are ready at this time in the evolution of your Soul Journey to receive the message. Your soul has evolved from a cell throughout the various forms of sentient beings, invented and mastered language, developed and destroyed countless civilizations, loved and learned, and you are now ready for Ascension.

Returning to the mysteries of the universe, many great philosophers discuss the idea that we have lived past lives. Today, many people claim to be able to remember these past lives. The Dalai Lama claims that he knows what body he is going to incarnate into next. In their tradition, each Dalai Lama is the incarnation of the last. Some people even use astrology and other signs in their lives to predict the nature, time and setting of their next life. And others argue, "No, you don't have past lives. You're just remembering your ancestors' lives."

However, the secret of the universe is not only that you have past lives, and you will have future lives, but you have lived this exact life an infinite number of times, doing it slightly different each time. Together, we are the sole source of all that is, what we may call God-consciousness, though even that term falls short of capturing the true essence of what we are. Through divine awareness, we experience every possibility, every individual life, and every soul journey of all sentient beings until we've experienced all that is, which is infinity.

The idea that heaven is something that will be experienced after this physical life is only partially true. The greatest answer to every question from the scientific and spiritual communities is "sort of yes, and sort of no." Did consciousness come from matter? Sort of yes... and sort of no. Did matter come from consciousness? Sort of yes... and sort of no. The following chapters reveal answers to the most crucial questions humans have ever asked.

Heaven, moksha, nirvana, and yoga are some of the words we use to describe the highest frequency that the Experience can be viewed from. It is not necessarily something that we achieve after we leave these physical bodies. Heaven is something that we may achieve now during this incarnation and every other incarnation. We can experience this frequency within every incarnation. This book explains what heaven looks like without using parables and allegories.

Now, before we begin, I will say that you can choose exactly what heaven on earth looks like for you, if that is even what you wish to experience in this incarnation. You are a divine entity experiencing all that is and can experience each lifetime through different frequencies and different vibrations. You can choose whether you want to live in heaven, hell, or some other variety in this version of the Experience. By the end of this book, you will clearly see the reality of all that is, reclaim total agency over your life, and see the invisible threads that connect one dimension to another.

This great revelation has always existed within you, a small light you have always known. What the Toltec people call "The Dream of the Planet" has only clouded our perception. Upon the initial taste of this wisdom, even in part, many people begin to struggle with nihilism – what Carl Jung calls the "Dark Night of the Soul" – and deep depression because it truly is ego-shattering and hard for our systems to digest.

The nature of darkness is twofold. First, there is primordial darkness associated with the essence of all that is. Having a relationship with this darkness is akin to Enlightenment. We will discuss this in detail as we move through the chapters. Second, there is the darkness responsible for fear, suffering, and delusion. This darkness is simply a blindness to the reality of who (or what) you are. When we mistake the impermanent for permanence, we allow external objects to define our inner reality. One who pierces the veil of the illusion by seeing with the eyes of their heart will harmonize with their physical eyes and learn how to define external objects by their inner reality.

The Great King Solomon realized this and, in the first line of his literature, proclaimed, "everything is meaningless," something that the Abrahamic religions have struggled to interpret for thousands of years. He was right, nothing has inherent meaning. And that truth is beautiful, because it means we are the ones who give everything meaning.

Let me say that one more time. Nothing has meaning; that is, nothing is "good" or "bad" in itself. And because of that, we can give meaning to everything through consciously analyzing and modifying our belief systems, as needed. This is the first step of the Awakening. The second step of the Awakening does not require conscious intervention – it is simply a state of being – but I will discuss that later.

A question I hear all the time is "How does one know they are enlightened?" The answer is simple: one is enlightened, not when their circumstances change, but when their response to circumstances changes, even if they don't experience the circumstances they would've preferred before enlightenment.

If you complain about anything at all, or have unforgiveness for yourself or someone else, or wish things would be different, you are not enlightened. As Don Miguel Ruiz Jr. said so eloquently, "Forgiveness is the moment you no longer wish the past were any different." When you realize that life has never happened to you, it is only happening through you, you begin to understand the reality of all that is. Everything you have ever experienced has always been for your good – it has always been an opportunity for you to experience all that is, and it is only your resistance to life that has caused suffering.

As someone who has lost people to untimely death and betrayal, someone who has been in fetal position so overwhelmed by the burdens of the world, I have compassion for all who suffer, but I am here as a living testimony of the Way. That said, in a perfect world, by the end of this book, you will forget I even exist and simply be present and blissful for the rest of your life. But first, I must teach you the difference between dissociating due to resisting trauma and truly living An Out of Body Life.

In this book, I will share my journey to Enlightenment (which is accessible to everyone, not just monks and High Priests), I will discuss the misconceptions (and Truth) of various Wisdom Traditions that actually all teach the same thing (Christianity/Judaism/Islam, Hinduism, Buddhism, Egyptian, Nordic, all the Theisms, and yes – even Atheism), and I will teach you how to never suffer again. You will learn the greatest Wisdom that I have ever been blessed with: How to Live an Out of Body Life.

The great wise yogis uncovered jnana (Sanskrit for "Knowledge") to explain the great mystery. And in fact, all the great wisdom traditions have been on to this. Each wisdom tradition offers significant insights and profound mysteries, collectively contributing essential elements to a larger conceptual framework.

Just as I began this book with the conclusion, so too did reality begin with infinity. You can think of it like all things existing all at once, just in potential form. And then suddenly all those things exploded into an infinite number of pieces. Each religion got a small piece, a small fragment, a small fractal of the great mystery of all that is. One person proclaimed, "This is true," another proclaimed, "That is true." Both being right and both being equally wrong.

As you turn the pages, you will begin to remember the great mystery of all that is; you will be able to ascend, you will be able to create, you will find bliss. You will forget what suffering is, and you will live An Out of Body Life.

THE FOUR
Levels of Truth

THE FOUR LEVELS OF TRUTH

PREPARE FOR LIFT OFF

T o help our minds receive this download, we can categorize the Truth into four categories: The Unspeakable, The Absolute Truth, The Relative Truth, and The Illusion.

The Four Levels of Truth can also be called the Four Levels of Reality because we can consciously choose to engage with what we call "Reality" at any of these levels at any moment. The purpose of Existence is, by definition, to Exist, which includes experiencing all the possibilities of every possible reality until all that is experiences is all that is. By understanding the Four Levels of Truth, we can recognize where we are in the Experience at any given time, and we can choose to shift into an alternative Experience of reality whenever we like.

The Unspeakable Truth

In the Great Mystery of all that is, we must take a moment to acknowledge the fact that words themselves are all made up. When humans, as we understand them, came into existence, there were no words. It is, in fact, a miracle that we can measure or understand anything at all.

In this noisy world, we take for granted the subtle fact that anything can be given meaning, that we can learn, perceive patterns, or even sense that what we experience isn't just a random combination of colors and noises and smells. And, at the deepest level, that we have five senses to begin with, or that perception itself is even a thing.

The next time you get upset about an argument, traffic, Global Warming, or whatever you feel is important, take a moment to just acknowledge the fact that it exists in the first place. Miracles aren't just when an Angel pushes your car out of the way of an accident – this entire existence is a Miracle! The Unspeakable Truth is the Level that existed before we started to catch on to what was happening. Therefore, the Unspeakable Truth cannot be explained with words or experienced with the five senses; it is just that – Unspeakable.

The term "language" simply means "tongue." It represents the words that come out of our mouths. The moment you say something, it is no longer Unspeakable. Words can never describe the Unspeakable level of reality, but they can point you in the direction.

There are two main ways that words can help you remember the Unspeakable level of reality, who you really are.

1. Anything you can see or think can't tell you who you are, but it can tell you what you are not. If you look around, anything that you see with your eyes is not you. This includes your body and anything you can experience with your senses. When you think a thought, you can say, "I am not that." Once you have said, "I am not that" to everything infinitely, what remains is what you are.

2. The second thing words can do is create comparisons. For example, you can say, "God is like silence," "God is like the little children," or "God is like peace, grace, and mercy." To describe all auspicious qualities infinitely could get you close to a fraction of the way of describing the Unspeakable truth.

Ultimately, you will see in this book that the Unspeakable Truth is something that cannot be directly described; it can only be experienced. Once you remember the Unspeakable Truth, there is no un-seeing it. Whatever you decide to do after experiencing true Enlightenment is done with complete Agency and without any suffering forever. We will get back to this Level of Reality by the end of the book, but for now, we will table it so we can navigate the rest of Reality.

The Absolute Truth

For all that is to experience all that is, It (what I will occasionally refer to as "God" just to simplify the concept into a term – but remember, "It" is Unspeakable) descended from the Heavenly realms down to the Earthly.

We could choose to simply exist with knowledge of the Unspeakable Truth for the rest of this incarnation and speak to no one, seeing everything as an illusion and meaningless (and many do once they are Enlightened). There is a lot of Wisdom in the decision to withdraw from the world, and that is a perfectly legitimate way to exist. Again, all possibilities of existence have already happened; "we" are simply exploring them.

There are also some who will choose to cause chaos in the Relative Truth realm and then mentally retreat to the Absolute Truth as a way to avoid dealing with it. Those who are not enlightened, who are only able to perceive the Illusion, will call those individuals "narcissists" or "manipulators." Those who are fully immersed in the Illusion without any understanding of Relative Truth or the Absolute Truth will choose to respond to afflictions by living in victimhood, or, alternatively, by "matching that energy" and becoming an unconscious manipulator themselves.

Those who operate at the Relative Truth level will begin to reflect on what causes someone to operate the way that they do. They explore childhood trauma, have compassion for the person, set strong boundaries, yet still harbor a small degree of animosity for the person, and probably gossip about them and celebrate the fact that they weren't sucked into that person's world.

The one who operates at the Absolute Truth level will remind themselves that the person is simply unconscious in the area they afflicted you. They know that everything happens for some reason and will remain at peace. These individuals spend very little time examining external objects and see every moment as an opportunity to examine themselves.

And the one who has experienced the breakthrough, who has tasted the Unspeakable Reality, will recognize that consciousness and unconsciousness are all constructed, that no one afflicted you, and that nothing happens for a reason. The One who exists at the Unspeakable Realm can't unsee the Reality of all that is. The fully Enlightened being knows nothing and is nothing and is only the witness of the Reality of all that is. Everything, operating perfectly.

The Level of the Absolute Truth remains true across all dimensions, soul journeys, timelines, cultures, and incarnations. To help understand the Absolute Truth, imagine a plain white canvas that changes color when you touch it with a paintbrush, or a finger, or breath, or any other item. The plain white canvas contains all the possible outcomes of what the portrait could look like. As any sentient being decides to paint on the canvas, the painting has already been completed in an infinite number of ways, but the being descends into the Relative truth to experience the act of painting, to live the art within.

The Relative Truth

Slowly but surely, all Creation began to descend into what we will call "The Experience."

Through time, all creations learned how to recognize patterns to survive. The more intellectual the life form, the more intention it has behind surviving. For example, Sunflowers have quite simple concerns: drink water and get sunlight, so they quickly learned how to grow always facing the sun. Mosquitoes, while seemingly brainless, often eat blood to deliver their babies. Ants have a cute feature about them: as humans experience Rapid Eye Movement (REM) during the dream state, ants experience Rapid Antenna Movement (RAM) where their antennas move around as if they were dreaming (though, since they lack a nervous system, it is likely that they do not dream – but, who knows?).

Humans are currently the most intellectual of beings. We invented complex symbols, noises, and systems to help all that is experience and understand all that is. The one whose Experience is at the Level of the Illusion only perceives the noises and systems, but they do not recognize the symbols. The symbols are outside their ability to interpret. The symbols were left as a bridge to bring us up from the Level of the Illusion to the Relative Truth, if you chose to experience this part of Reality.

When one person says that they saw an Angel, and another insists that Angels aren't real, they are both correct at the Relative Truth level. Unlike the Absolute Truth, which is Universally True under all circumstances, the Relative Truth is a matter of context, perspective, and belief of an individual sentient being. People can maintain completely opposite or contradictory beliefs and still be correct in their perspective. This is the level that compassion and honor can begin to come through.

After flipping the entire Mosaic Law upside down before the Israelites, Jesus said, "Unless you become like little children, you will not enter the Kingdom of Heaven." There will be many people who, because of the Illusion, believe that the Kingdom of Heaven is only going to be experienced when someone is separated from their body (what we call "death"). That person should know that Jesus also said, "The Kingdom of Heaven is not something that can be observed, nor will people say, 'Here it is,' or 'There it is,' because the Kingdom of Heaven is in you."

Heaven, as we will later explore, is impossible to access when someone is still identified with the Illusion, but one can begin to realize it at the Level of Relative Truth right now, not after Death.

The Illusion

The Level of Illusion is the total inundation into the Experience. Another word for the Illusion is Maya. We will discuss the Maya in depth in the next chapter, which is also called the Serpent in various wisdom traditions. Most people perceive the Experience at the Level of the Illusion.

In Western societies, we categorize belief systems into "religions" and "mythologies." Religions are said to be something that someone believes is real, whereas mythologies are said to be fiction that people do not really believe. However, that is because in contemporary English, we conflate the term mythology to mean fable or folklore. Mythology ultimately refers to a story that may or may not have happened, that points to a much deeper truth. Whether the story actually happened or not doesn't matter; only the moral does (unless someone is specifically telling the story with the claim that it is historically accurate).

All religions and wisdom traditions around the world contain various mythologies that answer some of the deepest questions humans have ever asked, such as the origin of the universe, morality, ethics, and many other important things. Without made-up words, there would be no stories, and without stories (whether made up or not), we would have no way of measuring anything.

From the perspective of preserving the human race, we would be at risk because we are not the physically strongest species. It is through our intelligence that we are able to survive, and it is through the databases of religion, culture, stories, and the like that have made us thrive as a species. The problem is that we fall in love with the stories and lose sight of the esoteric meanings. Worse, we even judge or persecute people who do not believe the stories that we tell, even if they haven't violated any of the principles within the stories (like murder, theft, etc.). We simply persecute people because they don't like the stories we like.

The Level of Illusion is so captivating because our society loves the idea that humans can be machines. We love a good movie about the neglected person who had some supernatural ability (like thinking or fighting) and used their machine-like bodies to take down an enemy. We romanticize people who don't have to study but just know things. I've met many people who identify with their neighborhood or city and pretend to have a certain way of living that is superior to others. This is all illusory.

From childhood, we are asked, "Who are your role models?" We are taught to identify with our mind and our body from a young age. We strive to mimic others. The problem is that we are not machines. We can respond and choose our programming.

A huge debate in modern society is the idea of determinism. There are currently three models of determinism.

Genetic determinism claims that your behavior and mood are determined by your genetics, grandparents, ancestors, etc.

Psychic determinism suggests that you're not necessarily the byproduct of your ancestors, but you are the byproduct of your parents and your upbringing (the way you were nurtured and initially in life). In this model, your genetics play a small or no role in your behavior and mood, but your upbringing plays the most important role.

Finally, **Environmental determinism**, which is that you are the product of your environment. If the economy goes up or politics go in your favor, everything is good. If you get a lot of likes on Instagram, you are happy.

A fun fact about me is that when I was younger, I was in a Hip Hop group, our studio was the closet of my friend's house. We lined the walls with a special foam that allowed us to record our music without any interference from background noise. Back then, I often talked about how I was a product of my environment. What I meant was that I identified with my community, taste of music, and belief systems. There was no distinction between who I was and what I had been through. It gave me comfort and a level of certainty to finally have an identity – after all, I, like many others, was not taught about my identity as I was growing up.

In summary, the Level of Illusion is when someone identifies with the mind, body, and experiences, and they allow their external world to determine the experience of their inner world. The Level of Relative Truth is when one has awakened from the Illusion and begins to choose one's own preferences for themselves. The Level of Absolute Truth is when someone has pierced through the veil and identifies with their Soul only and does not have preferences. Their only concern is spiritual growth. And finally, the Unspeakable level is the greatest of all, which we will unfold as we progress through this book.

The words we use are mere shadows of the shadow of all that is. We tend to create idols out of words, and then we worship them. We draw a word in the sand, say it, and then say, "This is the elite word, everyone must worship it!" But, before words, there was Word.

In Hebrew, the "Word" is the dabar. Dabar is the word used anytime God moves. When God speaks, walks, thinks, or does anything, it is always the dabar of God that performs the actions. Dabar comes from three Hebrew letters:

ד = Dalet, meaning "door"

ב = Bet, meaning "house"

ר = Resh, meaning "beginning" or "head"

In other words, when the unmanifested manifests through action, the higher purpose is that it opens a portal (or door) that connects the house of God (the world and all things that are manifested) to the unmanifested (the head, which is the Source of all that is).

We are already starting to descend, but let's stay as high as we can for a moment. The Dabar, the Word, existed as unmanifested and manifested all at once in the beginning. The word we use to describe everything is God. God is self-aware, but it experiences its awareness through the Dabar.

We are the action of God, the thoughts of God, the eyes of God, and all other words we can use. We are fractals of all that is, at the relative level. But, again, we always existed. So, we are the Experienced, that which is the faculty of Experiencing, and that which is Experiencing. In other words, we are all that is.

God, whether revealed as the sound Yahweh (YHVH), the one who saved the Israelites, or as Shiva or Krishna, who saved the Indians, or Zeus, who saved and murdered as he pleased - all of these are possible but not necessary. All wisdom traditions would agree that the Creator is beyond all words and actions. Whether God saved Israel or not is of no significance. When I was experiencing the Dark Night of the Soul, I found myself asking, "Who are you, who am I, and what do you want from me?" This is the answer I received.

There was no starting point in time. The Bible does an amazing job of describing this in John 1, which says, "In the Beginning, the Word was with God, and the Word was God. Through the Word, all things were made, and without the Word, nothing that was made would have been made. In the Word was life, and the life was a light to all living beings." This esoteric wisdom seems paradoxical until you examine it carefully. The scripture does not say, "He created everything," it says, "everything was created through Him."

The nature of creation can be thought of like fabric, and each appearance within the fabric (pants, shirts, etc.) is made possible by stitching. The stitching is made possible by thread. All the individual parts are the same material. In this example, the thread represents energy, which contains the potential for mind, intellect, and body. When the thread is stitched, it becomes a form or an appearance, which we call a "life." The potential of the mind, intellect, and body becomes manifested.

From beginning to end, from unmanifested to manifested, it is all the same fabric. You can't look at part of the fabric and say, "This is fabric and that is stitching," because they are one and the same. The stitching is simply an appearance within the fabric, but it is still the fabric. Whether you make a shirt, pants, or undergarments with the fabric, if the appearance of what was created was subsequently destroyed, the fabric would remain. However, if the fabric were removed, it would all disappear.

This is how consciousness works. It is impossible for something to be separate from consciousness. Consciousness is synonymous with existence, life, or God – It is all that is. Through It (whatever you prefer to call It), all things were made, and without It, nothing that was made would have been made. The reason that something cannot exist outside of Existence itself is that, by definition, it wouldn't exist. Non-existence can't exist. Additionally, everything that has existed, is existing, or will exist already exists. Non-existence can't become existence, and existence can't become non-existent. All Physicists will tell you that "energy cannot be created or destroyed; it can only be transferred or transformed into another form of energy." This is called the Law of the Conservation of Energy, and Spiritualists have no problem with this.

Lau Tzu famously said, "The longest journey a man must take is the eighteen inches from his head to his heart." What this is really saying is that the most challenging journey is to move from our egoic mind to our spiritual mind. From the Illusion to the Absolute Reality.

And this is the same whether you look at the study of matter or the study of consciousness. In Hinduism, the terms are Purusha (primordial consciousness) and Prakriti (form). Some Hindus practice Dvaita, which means consciousness and matter (form) are two separate realities. Dvaita means "two," from which we get the idea of duality. The other view is Advaita, which means "no two," from which we of course get the idea of non-duality. Non-duality states that there is no separation between consciousness and matter.

In the Bible, the Tree of Knowledge of Good and Evil represents duality. In the story, Adam and Eve ate from this tree, but truly this is a decision that every soul must make. If you eat from this metaphorical tree, you will feel separate from God. This is the path to the Illusion. It is through Illusion that one identifies with duality, or the Tree of Knowledge of Good and Evil. On the other hand, the Tree of Life represents non-duality because by eating from it, one maintains their awareness that they have always been One with all things.

The Maya, or the Illusion, is what causes us not to understand the difference between materialism and spirituality in the first place. Or more accurately, to believe that there is a difference between the two. There is no beginning and no end, there is no one or the other. Now, let us descend a bit more into the Illusion, or the Maya, of all that is.

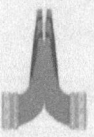

CHAPTER 1

THE SERPENT

CHAPTER 1: THE SERPENT

Every major Wisdom tradition, from all corners of the Earth, mentions a Snake in their doctrine(s). In Egyptian mythology, the Serpent is named Uraeus; in Alchemy, Ouroboros; in Norse mythology, Jormungandr; in Hinduism, they are the Nagas; in Abrahamic religions, Satan; in Toltec/Aztec/Mayan Traditions, Quetzalcoatl/ Kukulkan; and the list goes on. When you study each Tradition with an open heart, you realize that the Snake is always representative of the same thing: the *Swirling* Mind.

BUT DID YOU DIE?! – MR. CHOW

In the last chapter, we ended with a discussion about Maya, which we defined as the Illusion. To understand it more deeply, we must look at the original etymology in Sanskrit. The word Maya comes from the words Ma- meaning, "to measure" and Ya- meaning, "form/to give shape." Therefore, the word Maya means "to measure the form" or "to measure the shape."

The idea is that all things that have ever existed or ever will exist already happened all at once. They are above time and exist in a singular point we can call infinity. For the sake of compressing infinity into a commonly used word, let's call this God. In this definition of the word God, God is not the Universe,

God is the 0th dimensional, silent and androgynous entity that existed before anything unfolded. Time, space, and matter are contained in God, but it is not yet revealed because from the perspective of the beginning, time had not yet unfolded (though, all things including time existed within the infinite reality called God).

Maya, then, is not an illusion in the sense of it being completely made up. Maya is what occurs when God takes the time to experience itself in the form of time, space, and matter. As we said before, there is no beginning and no end to what we call reality. When we stop infinity in time, space, and matter, we do it so that we can experience all that is; so, we can measure the form of it; so, we can take our time to enjoy it and feel it. We measure the form and give a shape to the piece of infinity that we have stopped to view. This is Maya. Anything that is measurable is Maya.

Maya feels real at a Relative Level, but it isn't real at the Absolute Level. At the Absolute Level, there is no mind, body, energy or intellect. Once God decides to experience (and measure) a fractal of what it is, it takes on a mind, intellect, body, and energy, this is the Experience that I am referring to. The Experience includes all the possible realities of all that is, including form and formless beings.

As a father of four daughters, I have seen how much they all love the Barbie playhouses with all the various rooms in them. Imagine your inner child playing with a Barbie playhouse while sitting in a dark room, perhaps the attic. Now, imagine you shine a flashlight in one room and play there, that is equal to one incarnation. Within that room, you can create characters like Ken, Barbie and all their friends. You create rules of the game, identities (in some, Ken is kind, others he is ditsy), and eventually an entire story.

As you move from room to room, you can do this over and over starting from scratch each time, or you can carry over story lines into the next room. The challenge is that, while the characters may or may not be the same, the setting can be totally different in each room. Each room represents an incarnation.

Then, another day, you decide to come back into the same room and play the game differently, which you can do as many times as you like. This is the concept of parallel realities.

If the single playhouse has a connected theme, the journey through the rooms is what we call a soul journey. To have the full Experience, you dedicate your time and be present with each room.

As materialists point out, each of these playhouses are self-sustainable, meaning each of the movements by all the figures can be reduced to a series of mathematical equations. The characters don't need light to have a storyline. The storylines only existed as theoretical experiences (in Quantum terms, this illustrates Superpositions and explains the problem of Schrödinger's cat, which I will elaborate on in a future book). It isn't until the light shines on the house (and pervades throughout the entire house) that a particular theoretical storyline manifests.

Once the light has entered the room, it cannot change the appearance of the matter or flip chairs upside down or break any of the laws contained within the room (eliminating certain pseudoscientific theories from parapsychologists like Dean Radin, et al.). Before the light is shined upon the Dollhouse, it can be configured into anything the experiencer wishes to experience. But, once the light enters the Dollhouse, the rules of the game will remain the same, with very minimal exceptions.

The amazing thing about this light is that even if it illuminates dirty water, the light itself doesn't get dirty. Light doesn't mingle with anything that it lights up. The light simply illuminates each room, but it does not become the room. The light remains unchanged regardless of the room's condition or contents. This light is the pure consciousness which you are. It is unaffected because it exists in a different dimension than the Dollhouse.

While Maya describes the ability to measure all of existence, the Dimension in which measurement is taken is just as important. The word Dimension comes from the Latin word "dīmēnsiō," which also means "a measurement." So, Maya represents the infinite measurements that One can make. These are measurements of Itself, the entire system. These measurements are taken as each individual life.

The dimension One is measuring through depends on Its degree of focus within the Experience. Like a water molecule that moves faster or slower based on the temperature it is experiencing, the mind, body, intellect, and emotions experience Time relative to its level of focus.

When we have accumulated things that don't belong to our pure essence, time tends to move much faster. Stress, anxiety, bills, and other items within the system cause One to lose focus and time moves faster relative to the person's experience. This is the esoteric meaning of the Yoga term "tapas," which means "heat." Tapas is literally the burning away of impurities, which allows a person to prepare for meditation (where time ceases to exist). When we shake off the things that belong to the Illusion, our minds clear and we can live life with focus that enables us to perceive from higher dimensions.

So, Maya is the idea of measuring all that is, Dimension represents the frequency in which we are measuring all that is, and the measuring instrument is what we heretofore call "us."

Most of us identify with the limited instead of the limitless. We label ourselves based on a small sample size of Maya – Just one single room in the Barbie playhouse. To cling to anything would be like watching a millisecond of a movie and thinking you understood the entire movie. In other words, we get a glimpse of the Maya, the words, symbols and systems that humans created in the form realm and think that we fully understand God.

When my youngest daughter was an infant, I brought her to the Ocean for the first time. It was late at night; the waves were lit up by the moon and the stars (and some of the buildings in the distance). She absolutely loved it and quickly fell asleep in my arms to the peaceful noise of the waves crashing at my feet. Staring into the depth of the Ocean, I felt blissed out, practically worshiping it. Then out of the blue, a wave crashed into my leg, nearly knocking me over. It was then that I realized the true nature of the ocean. In my state of limerence, I had tricked myself into believing the Ocean was all-Loving and we had some special connection. Perhaps I watched too many Moana movies with my daughters. The ocean is deep and vast, and capable of killing you and ripping you to shreds. The ocean has no preference for whether one lives or dies. Fortunately, I did not have to find out Ocean's full capability that day.

The same way that we can have limerence for any object, we can have limerence for the idea of enlightenment. Sometimes, this gives us a puffed-up attitude and makes us think that we are better than other people, as if we can see things that others can't see. But true enlightenment is seeing the true nature of the ocean. It is really those who do not believe that there is anything beyond our five senses who are more "woo-woo" than those who do. To truly see with real Insight is to simply see things for what they really are.

If you think of the ocean, you may see stillness, small waves, giant waves, or anything in between. But what is the fundamental reality, the ocean or the waves? Do the waves contain the ocean or does the ocean contain the waves?

Some people would argue that the waves contain the ocean. We can clearly see that the water in the ocean is traveling by way of the waves that are carrying them, right? Well, we must take a closer look and ask philosophical questions to get to the bottom of this.

If the waves stopped moving, would the ocean still exist? Yes. But, if we took away the water, would the waves exist? Would little wave-ghosts still be there floating in the air? No.

Therefore, the Ocean contains the waves, not the other way around. The waves are not an illusion; we can clearly see them, but they are not the whole story of what is happening. Likewise, this is what life is like. Life as we know it is made up of individual souls completing infinite iterations of an infinite number of soul journeys.

There really is no beginning and no end, but for the sake of making this tangible to our level of consciousness, we can say that each soul starts off as a single cell. When ready, the single cell dies and then incarnates as something else, maybe an underwater plant for example. Once the soul leaves the plant (i.e. "death"), it incarnates as a coral reef, which is halfway between plant and animal. Once that soul has lived its life, it incarnates as an amphibian such as a frog, then a reptile, then a mammal, and eventually a human.

In a sense, Darwinism is somewhat true; however, species do not evolve into other species, rather the soul evolves into higher levels of sentient being as it grows within the linear view of this infinite reality (remember, we are taking an eternal model and viewing it linearly just so that our minds can understand this to some degree, however, this is only a small fractal of the bigger picture).

We do not have time to talk about timely versus untimely deaths and how the soul chooses when it is ready to leave a body and go into the next experience. But it is true to say that each soul experiences each species, each incarnation, infinitely until all possible outcomes are realized. Each one of these incarnations is like a small wave in the ocean of all that is. Each soul journey, through the different species that the single soul lives through, is like the tide that goes back and forth from the center of the ocean to the shore. Just as with the ocean, the soul journeys from cell to human and back to cell in reverse order.

There is a version of "you" that is experiencing an alternative version of Mother Theresa where she is actually very bitter, and another is experiencing a version of Hitler that created world peace, and etcetera infinitely. When I say, "a version of you," I am saying God, or all that is. Versions of you even experience different journeys in what we call the "after life," such as Angelic, extraterrestrial, and so forth. You experience the living states of awareness (awakened, sleeping, and deep sleep), as well as the post-living states of awareness (where we are existing outside of time, space, and matter). This is very abstract, so let's get back to practical language to make it more digestible. This is the kind of book that you can read multiple times to intellectually remember the details or read one time and totally open to the beauty of all that is once and for all, the choice is up to you!

The most detrimental part of identifying with anything, being a mom or a dad, a certain profession, being intelligent or creative, or even identifying with your current body or mind, is that you sacrifice your true freedom in return for a temporary label. Your true oneness with pure consciousness – God – pure expansion is lost amid trying to find grounding in Maya. We try to grasp a single wave, forgetting that we are the entire ocean.

The light in the flashlight is the perfect example of how the Illusion works. Modern science has studied light particles, which we call photons. The interesting thing about a photon that no one can explain is that photons, in themselves, are mass-less and color-less, yet we perceive all colors and can touch all mass because of photons (as well as quarks, atoms and possibly super strings. The deeper we get into Quantum Mechanics, the less things become tangible and the more they simply become a series of equations).

How can something that has no color because it is mass-less produce all the color that we see in a rose, rainbow, or an eye?

A photon cannot be seen when it is moving because it is limitless. In Einstein's famous equation $E = MC^2$, we can calculate the energy of any object by multiplying its mass times C (squared). C is a variable that stands for the Speed of Light, which is about 186,000 miles per second (300,000 meters per second).

A photon has no mass, so when you insert "$m = 0$":

We get $E = (0) \times 186,000$mps.

We all know that any number times 0 is 0, so then $E = 0$.

However, we know that photons *are* Energy, so the equation seems to not make sense. So, Quantum Theorists proposed the idea that light carries momentum and through that momentum, we can calculate its energy (this is known as the Planck-Einstein relation). It is like a wave that can push an object, though the wave is not an actual measurable object itself. How can no-thing push a thing? It is because of the momentum of the no-thing. From this, we can conclude that photons probably do not experience time. Light travels from its origin point to its destination immediately, so if you were an actual photon, you would not experience time.

The last Quantum Mechanics idea I will present before returning to the simpler ideas behind the nature of consciousness is the Heisenberg uncertainty principle. This principle states that you cannot simultaneously measure an object's momentum and its position.

Let's assume you are staring at one spot of a river for a few seconds, it would seem like you are looking at the same wave rippling through some branches, but in truth, millions of particles have crossed your eye's view, and it is not actually the same wave. Heraclitus famously said, "No man ever steps in the same river twice."

If you've ever had limerence for a person based on a single glance, or even for a glance that lasts a few years or more, and then one day you noticed that it seems like that person changed, it is because every single breath they took, they were most literally a different person. You only thought that they were the same person because of the illusion of Maya.

To understand these higher dimensions, there are theoretical equations we can use, but none of this is agreed upon by Quantum Theorists. When we stop a photon, we can finally see it, so we are making the limitless limited. When we stop a human to observe them, sure we can measure their current position, but we will never understand that human's momentum. At best, we can know the body and 1% of the mind of another person. But the other 99% of them will be unknown forever.

This is the same on an atomic level where protons, neutrons and electrons only make up 1% of an entire atom and the rest of the atom is Dark Matter. This holds true on a cosmic scale where planets, stars, and other celestial bodies only make up 1% of the Universe, but the rest is also Dark Matter.

This is true at the Relative Level as well. You will never know someone's inner world, and no one will ever know yours. This is all Maya. Maya is the light, whether it is moving or stopped, Maya even includes the things that do not exist. Maya exists at the level of the mind, but the mind is only an object in the entire Experience. We will go much deeper into the difference between you and the mind in the coming chapters.

For now, let's deeply explore the mind and the Illusion of the Planet. In most Wisdom Traditions around the world, you will see some sort of serpent. In Egyptian mythology, it is named Uraeus, in Norse mythology, it is Jörmungandr, in Alchemy, it is called Ouroboros, and in Judo-Christian religions, the serpent is called Satan.

The serpent is the mythological character of the Illusion of the Planet. The illusion of the planet is anything that causes a sentient being to lose its purity. Purity simply means to only contain the substances that are truly you. If you add dirt to a cup of water, the water is no longer pure; not because the water sinned (as we incorrectly deduce in some religions), but because the water is now polluted with a substance that isn't its own.

In Sanskrit, the word Samsara' describes a person who has bought into the Illusion of the Planet. Samsara translates as "wandering," "world," or "running in circles." There is a huge distinction between the Earth and the World. The Earth is simply a rock in space, but the World includes everything in the known Universe, including matter and energies. The intention behind the Bible verse that says, "Satan, who is the god of this world, has blinded the minds of those who don't believe" (2 Cor. 4:4) is to point out another level of awareness that exists above the mind.

This is a good time to correct a limitation in the religion of Christianity. Christians interpret the Greek word "metanoia" as repentance. The widely accepted misinterpretation is that "meta" means "to change" and "noia" means "mind." The romanticized version of this means that we were born as impure in ourselves and we need to "repent" (often in the form of self-harm or self-denial) so that we can attain purity. This interpretation is flawed

42

as it misses the root cause of suffering. People try to "pray away" certain things that others deem as impure, but they have no idea what purity looks like within themselves. They try to change their mind and alter themselves to become socially acceptable, and it never lasts. It leads to self-judgement and self-denial, which in turn leads to the judgement of others and the denial of others.

Here's the solution. The same Greek word meta is used in the word metaphysics, but it does not mean "to change physics." Meta is more accurately translated to "above" or "beyond," so just as metaphysics is "above physics," metanoia should be translated as "above the mind." In the context of Sanskrit, this would be above the wandering mind – Above the serpent.

This is such a profound thing to really understand. When we try to morph ourselves into something based on the Illusion of the Planet, we will only perpetuate suffering. In an effort to try to change the mind, we never learn how to simply be with our minds. It is like the saying "don't fight fire with fire," we often try to fight our minds with our own minds.

We must realize that the mind is the very thing we need to Experience all of this in the first place. And, when we learn how to nurture the mind, suddenly we recognize that the only thing that has ever existed is Heaven. We are only having a dream that we are not in Heaven.

In history, many scientists and philosophers have conducted experiments across all five senses of our body (plus virtual reality tests, which would suggest a sixth sense of being) that demonstrate how the Illusion works scientifically. Anil Seth, an incredible thought leader and neuroscientist, has a Ted Talk called "Your Brain Hallucinates Your Conscious Reality," where he explores many different 2D optical, 3D virtual, tactile and audio illusions that demonstrate that what we call reality is simply a projection of the mind.

Anil mentions this famous optical experiment from 1995, where Edward Adelson showed  how our minds negotiate what we call reality. In this illustration, while it appears that the A and B squares in the image to the left are different shades of gray, you can see in image on the right that they are in fact the same shade. Our mind (via our eyes) perceives two "realities," but our Intellect (via knowledge) can now reason that there is only One.

In Anil's talk, he says, "Right now, billions of neurons in your brain are working together to generate a conscious experience – and not just any conscious experience, your experience of the world around you and of yourself within it... We are all hallucinating all the time; when we agree about our hallucinations, we call it 'reality'."

The Dream feels so real because it has infiltrated our mind to the extent that we believe it is us narrating the Dream. If you take a second to listen, you will notice that the voice is our parents' voice in our head, our childhood friends who revealed our insecurities, our fears about business, government and jail that didn't come from our own mind, etc. The fears and desired freedoms, the pursuit of happiness, and all those other concepts exist only in Samsara. The good news is that Samsara only exists in the future and the past, it does not exist right now. To shut the mind off, to escape Samsara, the only requirement is to be in the Highest Dimension, called now.

The Old Testament breaks down 613 laws to explain the swarm of thoughts. So much thinking, so much judgement, so much fear. Why? Because we are looking for others to tell us right from wrong. This is the Tree of the Knowledge of Good and Evil. It looks like it will taste good.

Let's take the story of the Garden of Eden as an example. The first two humans, named Adam and Eve, were told that they could eat from the Tree of Life or the Tree of the Knowledge of Good and Evil. The former would sustain them forever, whereas the latter would result in them gaining secret heavenly wisdoms, which would result in death. The couple couldn't resist as they were tempted towards the Tree with the Knowledge of Good and Evil. When they ate the Forbidden fruits, they immediately felt shame, hid from God, and eventually died.

In the first few chapters of the Book of Genesis, God tells Adam that he may eat from any of the fruits in the entire garden, except he must not touch the fruit with the knowledge of good and evil or he would surely die. The tree with the knowledge of good and evil was one of two trees in the middle of the garden. The other one was the tree of life.

In Genesis, the serpent told him that he would not actually die. Instead, when Adam would open his eyes, he would possess the knowledge of good and evil, just like God. When Adam finally ate from the tree of knowledge of good and evil, which as God said, would result in his death, he did not actually die a physical death.

Instead, God talked to Adam again and told him that he would now have to labor for the rest of his days. His wife Eve was told that she would experience menstrual cycles. Eve is representative of the feminine side of all humans while Adam is representative of the masculine side (Part 2 of this Book Series, called The Kingdom and the Garden, goes deeply into the esoteric meaning of Adam and Eve and how they actually represent both sides of every human, not two separate humans). The final consequence of Adam becoming impure was that there would be an enmity, or an intense hostility, between Adam and the serpent, which represents the ego of humans. In other words, if Adam made his decisions based on external noise, Adam would suffer his own mind.

Since, despite eating the forbidden fruit, Adam did not die physically, this shows the idea of Christ consciousness is not about physical death. If that were so, then when the man Jesus, or Yeshua, died, humans would no longer physically die. They would live eternally in the bodies that they were born in. This is because the death that Adam, and the rest of creation, suffers is not a death of the body, but of the mind, a perceived separation from God. Adam fell away from understanding his Oneness with God through the knowledge of good and evil, the serpent, the Samsara. The same story that is in Christianity, Judaism and Islam is the same story in every other wisdom tradition around the world.

To take it a step further, during the revelation of Christ consciousness (the New Testament), the people constantly bring up something called the Mosaic law, which Jesus continually refutes. The Mosaic law is the egoic law, it's the idea of humans making things up. Some of them aren't so bad, like honoring mother and father, not lying, etc., but some of them are about killing people. Some of the stories of the Old Testament are insane and it's no wonder people are so turned off by the Bible. It's not just the "radical Christians," it's the actual reading of the Old Testament. It's nuts, even the New Testament still has ego sprinkled in there. Women can't teach, and all the other nonsensical jargon. The whole point of Jesus' message is to stop going outward for your direction, now is time to go inward. Chapter 14 of the Book of Romans concludes with a significant verse, which states,

> "Whatever you believe about these things (the law) keep
> between yourself and God. Blessed is the one who does not
> condemn himself by what he approves. But whoever has
> doubts is condemned if they eat, because their eating is not

*from faith; and everything that does not come from faith is
sin."*

It couldn't be any clearer than that. This is the same theme
with every wisdom tradition, and where theism and atheism hold
hands. True theism is not about serving an external god, a man-
made idol in the sky. Atheism refutes all man-made gods also.
God is all. God is not separate. As soon as you separate God and
measure it within the Maya, you have created an idol, which is
only a small fractal of God. This is a fine path to come to Oneness,
but it is only Relative truth, not Absolute, and certainly not the
Unspeakable Truth.

Attachment to pleasure also means attachment to pain. You
cannot have one without eventually experiencing the other. The
Shiva Sutra helps us understand this by saying, "Pleasure and
pain are considered to be something external" to the Enlightened.
Commentaries by Ranjit Chaudhri expand on this and say,
"pleasure and pain are unavoidable... however, pain does not
have to cause suffering. Suffering is due to our thoughts about
pain. We believe pain is bad, pain should not be happening to us,
and our negative thoughts about pain cause suffering. Non-
acceptance of pain leads to suffering. On the other hand,
experiencing pain without passing judgement on it eliminates
suffering." Now, let us explore the next layer of reality.

The Naked Yogi

CHAPTER 2: THE NAKED YOGI

Light is not the fundamental reality. Darkness makes up 99% of what we call "real." Noise and sound occur as temporary phenomena, but when they are finished, the only thing that remains is something much deeper than the noise: The Darkness. In this Chapter, we will discuss the darkness.

SILENCE IS THE LANGUAGE OF GOD – RUMI

I n the last chapter, we discussed the 1% of all existence, the light that illuminates creation and allows us to experience all that is. In this chapter, we will discuss the remaining 99%, the darkness that rests behind the temporary phenomenon we call light.

As you read this book, you will hear your inner voice translating all the words. However, in between every single thought, every single sentence, and if you pay attention to the subtleties of life, every single word, you will realize the silence of all that exists. Resting in the background of every noise, every smell, every photon of light is a vast nothingness. Since all atoms are 99% nothing, it is said that if you were to remove the nothingness from every atom in the human body, the only mass that would remain would be the size of a piece of sand. Most people identify with the light they can see, and they remain in samsara; however, this chapter will help you identify with the deeper element that you are: The silence.

Imagine being the first humans on Earth. Whether we evolved from cellular form through different sentient species to finally become human or if we just appeared as human at the very beginning really is of no consequence. But imagine being the first humans on Earth.

Imagine that there were just a dozen humans to start. Imagine that no one had seen their own reflection, so nobody knew what they looked like. When a human looked at another human there was no reason to assume they were looking at something that looked like them. There was no fundamental distinction between humans and animals in the first humans' minds. How could they know if they themselves were a tree or an animal looking at a human? There were no words, no mirrors, no way of knowing what sentient or insentient meant. There was certainly no concept of "cute" or "ugly" just yet. So, the original human had no idea that it looked like the other.

On a quick note, when we're walking in public and say "hi" to someone who doesn't say "hi" back, we might try to assess what is wrong with that person. But that is all because of the Illusion that we think that this person is human, and that means they are like us. But what if those people were insentient beings that were only placed in your path to reveal more of yourself?

What if each person that you encounter was only God presenting you with a new opportunity to experience more of yourself?

Instead of assuming that people should be some type of way or trying to figure out what's wrong with everyone, we may consider approaching each moment as an opportunity to remain in ourselves. The first step to living An Out of Body Life is to live a life inside of ourselves, inside of our own experience, our own meditation, seeing our whole life as meditation, as a ceremony.

If someone doesn't reply with a "hi", most people would think, "that person is mean." The intelligent ones would assume, "That person must be having a bad day." The wise, however, would raise a question to themselves, "What is this person reflecting back to me?" They might discover that they have a fear or rejection or an unmet need to be seen and validated. They might thank the shadow of the person who didn't say "hi" back because they provided them with an insight into their own belief systems.

Rather than stepping into victimhood or judgment (the "drama triangle" in modern psychology terms), the wise will take that moment as an opportunity to examine and potentially redefine their belief system to find peace in not being acknowledged in that moment. Rather than choosing not to say "hi" to the next person that crosses their path, the wise will simply embody the energy from their new belief and forget all about the moment. The wise will choose to be present in the next moment, and they may or may not say "hi" to the next person they come across. Remaining in a constant state of self-inquiry is an entry level step into living An Out of Body Life.

Now, back to the original human. There are two great theories on the nature of the first humans.

Aristotle held the famous belief that the first humans were "hoi tuchontes," or "ordinary humans." He suggested that the first humans had no intelligence, they were just kind of here. The first humans, in this case, had a capacity that was greater than animals (though not far apart), but they hadn't stepped into the fullness of their intelligence, so they were of no account. They may have lived a full life (or gotten eaten by a dinosaur) but accomplished nothing extraordinary; nothing really happened. They never communicated, learned very little, discovered nothing, and they were just kind of like animals existing, and there was nothing special about them at all.

The second theory is opposite of this theory; it suggests that the first humans were more intelligent than those living at the time of you reading this book. This position holds that the earliest humans were so connected to intuition and to Mother Earth (which they considered to be God) that the language they created was essentially a bunch of onomatopoeias that made more sense in the context of what they were going through. They were so intuitive because they were not diluted and clouded by the Illusion of the Planet or the Illusion of Self. They knew how to move their bodies naturally, they spoke only when they needed to, they did not use filler words, their "yes" meant yes, and their "no" meant no.

Each of these theories of the original human is so powerful because whether we started off as knowing nothing and evolved into our intelligence, or if we started off as all intelligent and then developed an ego and slowly fell away from that, there was some kind of progression or digression involved from the earliest human until the ones we are now. This chapter explores who we are as mind, body, and energy, and then ponders what we could be if all of that were stripped from us.

One Sunday afternoon in 2018, I was sparring in Muay Thai and suddenly slipped into an out-of-body experience. I was throwing jabs and dodging oncoming punches and kicks when suddenly time slowed down and my awareness deepened. My awareness shifted from perceiving reality through my eyes to looking down at my body as I was sparring. I saw myself fighting as if I was my consciousness at the top of the ceiling, looking down, and I could see myself out of my body. While all this was happening, I couldn't feel any of the punches or kicks (it's pretty common not to feel strikes during sparring anyway, since there's so much adrenaline, but this time it felt really strange). I also remember my mind being on autopilot, simply observing as my body fought instinctively.

Nothing special happened in the sparring session, but it felt really cool to experience. I've always been the type to have a mystical experience and then reject it or try to rationalize it, so my first thought was, "Maybe I got hit so hard, I was hallucinating." But, even if that was true, regardless of the catalyst that caused me to be out of body, I was still in such a state, so it didn't matter how I got there. The fact that I could perceive my sparring session in that 30-second window from above my physical body was enough to show me that there is more than what we call physical reality.

After this sparring session, I came up with the title of this book, An Out of Body Life – it's taken me about eight more years to finally write down everything I wanted to cover in this book.

"IT ISN'T YOU VERSUS HIM, IT IS YOUR JIU JITSU VERSUS HIS JIU JITSU"

A few months later, I found myself competing at a Jiu-Jitsu tournament, and I was feeling a lot of anxiety. I had a great coach who gave me the perfect advice. He said, "No matter what happens at the end of this jiu-jitsu tournament, do not allow yourself to be identified by the outcome. If you win, don't become cocky, and if you lose, don't be depressed. **It isn't you versus him, it is your Jiu Jitsu versus his Jiu Jitsu.**"

I used to identify with my performance and adrenaline would kick in as soon as I began and I would get nervous and have adrenaline dumps. If I lost, I felt this sense of self-loathing but if I won, I felt really cocky. As I left the tournament, I'd either play 50 Cent if I won or a gospel song to cope with losing, there was no gray area! And so, based on my coach's advice, I stopped identifying with my mind and my body in a fight scenario and the competitive arts when I was in front of other people and all eyes were on me. This was a great training ground for detaching from my mind and body. For becoming a naked yogi.

To be naked is to simply take off all the ego, culture, titles, and definitions that we give ourselves. And yoga means "union." So, the naked yogi is simply one who is deeply connected to – one with – their purest self.

Growing up, the idea of purity never settled well with me because I was raised around judgmental people who told me how I needed to be and what purity was for them. They imposed their belief systems on me, and I didn't like that at all. What I came to understand is that purity is simply the essence of something without anything added to it. If I put dirt in a glass of water, that water is no longer pure. So, to add anything to myself is to be impure. How many times have we done this in our lives? The way we dress, the profession we take, the ideal of being a good father or husband, how to speak, think, etc. We even get our morality from others. But that creates impurities inside of us.

The reality is that since we are all emanations of God, we are all different. And, since we are all different, what is pure for one person is impure for another. For example, I know many people who eat meat. To them, there is no difference between eating a plant or eating an animal because plants and animals are equally alive. So, unless someone can live solely on sunlight (breatharian), something must die for them to live. Their logic is sound. For that person, they show reverence for the animal before they consume it; therefore, eating animals is pure for them. There are others who, through a different form of introspection, choose to eat only vegetables, and to them that is pure.

Both individuals did serious soul-searching and choose to live life the way their soul requires, so both individuals in this example are pure. Some people celebrate an individual day of the year and consider it holy, and others consider every day equally sacred, and they celebrate them all. They are both living pure lives – both are uninfluenced by others in choosing the expression of living that works for them.

There are many people who do not have their own opinion, so they simply follow their parents, religion, or friends. They rely on external objects to tell them how to manage their own faculties. This person blows with the wind in whatever direction it moves. Sometimes, a person like this has a unique path that allows them to fit in various cultures. To them, it makes no difference if they are in wealthy neighborhoods or ghettos; they can do just fine.

Many people thrive off being in diverse cultures and trying new things without any attachment to their surroundings. If that openness and flexibility is the root of their decision not to decide, then to them, that is also pure. However, others simply do not choose because they are afraid of being judged or ostracized, this is where purity can become defiled. This is where the soul can become corrupted, and the mind can become scattered. Being in perfect Yoga with one's Self is a matter of the mind, body, intellect, and energies being fully naked of foreign objects.

One of the greatest Illusions in our culture that we pretty much say every single day is, "I had a thought" or "I ran that mile" or "I lifted that weight" or "I achieved the success" but **the truth is that *you* haven't thought a single thought your entire life** – your mind has thought all of the thoughts. The mind is like an earth suit that allows consciousness (light, or God) to Experience all that is. If the mind did not exist, there would be no Experience. Therefore, the mind is like the glue between the seen and the unseen. The mind is the part of the whole that takes in Maya.

The unconscious mind consistently attends to sources of attraction and aversion, perceiving itself as central to one's experience of reality. Most people are enslaved to the mind; they don't realize it's simply an accessory to the Experience, so they become subservient.

THE TRUTH IS THAT YOU HAVEN'T THOUGHT A SINGLE THOUGHT YOUR ENTIRE LIFE

They do everything they can to satisfy the demand of the tyrannical mind because they fully identify with it. The mind is to the Soul what the Maya is to the Unspeakable: It reflects the higher truth, but it is not itself the higher truth. This is the same with the body, energies, and intellect. This next section will help you explore purity within your own faculties based on specific things that tend to get in the way.

As we said in the beginning, the purpose of this book is not to find something outside of your Self to evolve into. This book will help you realize you are already perfect in every way. Together, we will look at the things that have been inhibiting your ability to see this for yourself. There are only four ways that the Self at the Relative Level can remain partially tied to the Illusion. Either the mind, body, intellect, or energies can be pulled into the Illusion of the Planet.

The Mind. The mind in this context can be divided into three parts: memory (the past), perception (the present) and imagination (the future). This is the part of you that can wander and flicker from thought to thought all day.

A recent study by Psychologists at Queen's University in Kingston, Ontario, using fMRI scans, revealed that the average person has about 6,200 thoughts per day. In the Atlanta Airport near my home, there are roughly 2,000 flights per day. To cling to a random thought out of the 6,200 we have per day would be like hopping on a random flight out of Atlanta Airport over a three-day period and ending up wherever that flight takes you. Some people live their entire lives like this. Flying from thought to thought. Others get so overwhelmed that they choose none of the flights (thoughts) and travel nowhere in their lives. Whether highly active or inactive, most people are simply tormented by their minds all the time, even in their dreams.

The thing about the mind that most people don't realize is that it doesn't exist in the present. How do you get the mind to go away? Be present. People love alcohol and other substances because they intuitively know that it brings them into the present moment. When someone is drunk on alcohol or high on weed, suddenly, they don't care about the bills anymore. The argument they had with their spouse suddenly doesn't matter to them anymore. The only problem is that alcohol or substance induced Yoga is only temporary. Once it wears off, there is an incredible price to pay. Not only does it have a significant impact on the Mind, but it also results in suffering for the Body and Energies (which we will discuss next).

When most people aren't intoxicated, they are often fully consumed with their past or future, which means their mind is entirely online, and they continually suffer. To some, an inner voice keeps jabbing them to worry about the future; otherwise, they will be unsuccessful and let everyone down. So, they base their entire lives on avoiding failure. Others are trapped in the past. They feel guilt or shame over a past action or thought. Their lives revolve around trying to heal that wound, yet this effort only reinforces the pain and often causes them to project that same wound onto others.

The solution for a person with the problem of a highly active or inactive mind is simply focus. There are many ways of achieving peace in the mind. Remember, your natural state of mind is peace. It is only due to things that have been added to your mind that you do not realize peace every moment of every day.

First, notice I did not say that your natural state of mind is happiness. In America, one of the so-called inalienable rights in the Declaration of Independence is "the Pursuit of Happiness." Anyone who pursues happiness will not find it because it is not something to be pursued. The implication is that if you chase a specific thing, whether that be a career, money, or fame, you will finally discover happiness when that thing arrives. While this phrase is well-intentioned, it causes a scattered mind and makes peace unachievable.

Peace is not to be pursued, nor can it be achieved through repetition of a spiritual practice.

The New Age spiritual community preaches a similar doctrine, the Doctrine of Manifestation, which can also lead to a scattered mind if not practiced properly. Most people really preach the Power of Obsession, not Manifestation. Again, this teaching is rooted in the idea that we are simply unhappy and require an outside object to find happiness. Practitioners of the Manifestation movement teach different mantras, spells, and rituals that they claim produce abundance. While they very well may bring some material results, they don't necessarily provide peace of mind. It doesn't matter how much money or fame you have, or how good your boyfriend is to you, or whether you have the child you've prayed for, etc. If you have not found happiness without these external validations, then accumulating them will only intensify the unhappiness that already exists within you. Rather than attempting to manifest things externally, the peace that every person is seeking is found through manifesting inwardly.

There was a wise sage who would take questions from his students. One student, who learned a specific set of mantras and rituals, went to the sage and asked, "How many repetitions am I required to complete to be Enlightened?"

The wise sage simply replied, "Enlightenment isn't a matter of repetition, but of realization."

This is what focus truly is. Focus, or the ability to hold one thought at a time, happens when one realizes that they are separate from the mind. Strangely enough, when one realizes they are not the mind, they experience true union with the mind. The mind no longer wages tyrannical battles but instead serves the One that has descended in order to experience it. So, how does one settle down the mind?

Music and dance provide beautiful ways to temporarily achieve focus. When all our energy is poured into singing a familiar song or worshipping God, all our thoughts suddenly disappear. A life of devotion can help one ease the mind and learn to surrender into every moment. When one surrenders into every moment, the mind doesn't afflict them because the scattered mind dissolves in the present moment.

Like alcohol and other substances, music and dance can provide temporary relief from our tyrannical minds; however, to truly settle the mind down, we must look at a place that very few spend time with: our ethics and values. A person who has a scattered mind often has scattered behaviors simply because they don't know what is pure for them. They vacillate between wanting to be single and wanting to be in a relationship, from fasting from social media to rationalizing why they need to update their status, etc. This person is uneasy more than they are at peace. This is one place where Religion can help at first. In Abrahamic religions, there are 10 commandments that are actually very similar to the 10 commandments of Yoga.

Yoga 10 Commandments	Moses 10 Commandments
Do not harm	Be devoted to all that is
Do not lie	Don't identify with anything
Do not steal	Honor the names of God
Do not overindulge	Rest
Do not identify with anything	Honor your ancestors
Be clean/pure	Do not harm
Be content	Do not cheat on your partner
Be self-disciplined	Do not steal
Study yourself	Do not lie
Be devoted to all that is	Be content

Notice that these are remarkably similar to each other, but they may not align with what is pure for you. Or perhaps your interpretation of these differs from the religious interpretation. It does not matter – what matters is that you have a single-minded focus, and a great path to achieve that is to write down your values. Otherwise, lacking clarity about what you value can lead you to getting caught in what the Toltec people call 'the Judge' and 'the Victim' mentalities. It is often due to distraction and an unclear mind that we begin to judge ourselves either solely based on what others expect or on our desire to rebel against it. Rebellion is truly a beautiful thing when One is aware. When one is fully in touch with their Self, there is no other voice. **One of the greatest achievements is to have a single thought at a time.**

The Body. The body in this context is your physical body, also called the food body in Indian philosophies. We are talking about your head to toes and all the organs, bones, veins, and arteries in between. The body can also be divided into three parts: Memory (what you put into your body), Expression (your ability to move your body), and Service (what you do with your body).

When most people think of memory, they only associate it with the mind. However, your body has memory, and so does everything that you put in it. Every cell in your body, every DNA and RNA strand, every microbiome, etc., has its own memory.

Scientists have proven and can easily calculate the memory of the body. Not only that, but everything that you eat and drink has memory as well. Due to concepts like Natural Selection, diverse types of sentient beings have different memory capacities. And, depending on the being's life experience, their memory capacity was either fully utilized or not; its descendants' memory capacities are adjusted accordingly. Each of these memories ties us to the Illusion of the Planet in a different way than the mind. While the mind impedes our ability to see ourselves as perfect

65

through its scattered nature, the body can become an impediment through impurities.

Aquatic beings, trees and plants, insects and reptiles, birds, land animals, and humans all have different memory capacities. When one consumes the other, the body must integrate the memory that it consumed, process it, and eventually become one with the new memory. It is simple for the body to memorize a 2-step dance, but an entire choreography requires work.

Imagine performing a choreography in a genre that you don't prefer, or to a song that's off-key. This is like eating foods that are not meant for your body. Ideally, to achieve peace in the Body, the best option is to consume foods with less memory, such as fruits, vegetables, and nuts. If you must eat meat, the best option is to eat fish or other aquatic beings, which have accumulated less memory to process with the computer you call a physical body.

Not only what you eat, but how you eat can also play a vital role in the purity of your body. How often do we find ourselves eating while walking or completing another task? Or not thoroughly chewing our food? Or eating in a state of stress? The consequence? The food requires more work from our bodies, slowing down our operating system. Eating slowly, in a state of gratitude, in an upright position, and only as much as we actually need is a good start to finding union in the body. One who gets their nutrition and eating posture in order is on to a good start of purifying their bodies. If you have the time, then cooking your own meals over a fire is another way to purify your body. Just as

Religion can provide one with a good baseline of values and ethics, it can also give an example boilerplate for the types of foods and the way to consume those foods. The Ayur Vedas are the best (found mostly in the Atharvaveda and Rig Veda) for a starting point.

Regardless of the written models of eating and digestion, the most important thing is to have a relationship with your own body. Ask your body, "Body, what would you like me to provide you with? How can I serve you better?" When you are in union with your body, it is much easier to understand its language. Otherwise, you may confuse a bowel movement for hunger or hunger for thirst, or a call to fast for a call to work out.

The body is a highly complex system, and the idea of purifying your Self begins with how you manage the system. Again, purity is not about fitting a cookie-cutter model; it is about being pure within your Self.

The Naked Yogi is not merely naked of thoughts but is also pure within those thoughts. If you were able to only perceive one thought at a time, but that thought was just someone else's, you are not yet fully naked. Purifying your body is a method to Experience all that is in the most profound way possible.

Taking care of the body is the first step of purifying it – the next is what you do with the body in daily life. This is much deeper than just setting up a workout regime (which we will not discuss in this book, but it is also crucial for some people). When I say what you do with your body, I am referring to your vocation, the way you spend your time. Many people believe that karma determines whether their lives will be easy or full of hurdles, and that doing good deeds ensures good rewards while bad deeds bring negative consequences. Although this holds true to a certain degree, the concept of karma goes much deeper. The problem with working to achieve or avoid something is that we are still attached to the outcome. This is only another form of samsara.

When we deeply explore our core beliefs, we may find that we often consult with our unconscious ego in deciding how to spend our time. We do things that we like well, but the things we do not want to do cause suffering. Sometimes we find ourselves in a career or a relationship that we do not like anymore, and we feel stuck, so our bodies get lethargic, and our minds feel depressed. This is because we are not utilizing our bodies in a way that we enjoy.

We stay in the cycle of Samsara due to attraction and aversion. The reason we remain in Samsara is that we are doing things for ourselves under the illusion that we are separate from others. We believe that we are in a rat race and must acquire money, power, or fame to survive and thrive. There are three ways we can use our bodies and benefit from it – two of them are still within Samsara, and the final way is the way out.

The first way is to strive for our goals, focus on what we enjoy, avoid what we dislike, and stay invested in the results. In America, we say "see it to the end." Occasionally, this can go very well for us. This approach has contributed to success in business for many individuals. Countless CEOs proudly live this way, and that is wonderful for them. However, there are others who were not so fortunate. So many CEOs got rich this way and then lost it all quicker than a shooting star falling across the sky. A huge portion of them fell into depression, got divorced, went through substance abuse, or even committed suicide. When someone is attached to the outcomes of their work, they become enslaved to the faceless god of capitalism. If they do well, they feel well; if they do unsatisfactorily, they feel bad.

The second method is similar to the first, except there is no attachment to the outcomes. This person focuses on what they enjoy and avoids what they dislike, does their absolute best, and isn't attached to the outcomes. This might seem like the best way to live; however, it is still Samsara. If someone can keep this up forever, then it isn't so bad, but most people will burn out if they don't eventually see results in what they are doing. The very fact that they are avoiding what they dislike is evidence that they still have a little ego steering their life. In fact, it may be entirely ego disguised as Spirit. Even if a person can commit to this way of living for the rest of their life, they will most likely neglect certain important things because they simply do not want to do them.

The third way to use the body is the path to Enlightenment. The One who lives a pure life has no preference to what they are doing daily, they simply do what needs to be done. This is the path of selfless service. In this path, we no longer do things with our Self in mind. The veil of separation is dissolved, so when someone on this path serves another, they know that everyone is being equally blessed. Likewise, if the Other suffers, they feel suffering for them also. The path to purifying the body is to use the body in a way that serves others with no attachment to outcomes. The selfless servant derives his or her energy from the infinite, rather than the finite Maya. The selfless servant doesn't feel lethargic due to procrastinating from things they were trying to avoid or "do later" – they simply do what needs to be done. For clarity, that absolutely includes naps, if the person needs that – the selfless servant knows that one cannot give what one does not have. When we learn how to take care of our bodies through diet, exercise, mindfulness, and servitude, we solve the problem of purity and get one step closer to becoming a Naked Yogi.

The Intellect. The Intellect is much different than the mind and is much subtler than intelligence. While the mind can be scattered and flaky, the Intellect moves more delicately. Intelligence describes the act of accumulating added information in the present or future, but the Intellect is the faculty that can discern truth from falsehood – it sifts through intelligence, as necessary, and holds the worldview of the individual. Intelligence can drive someone insane, but the Intellect can revive and bring one from death to immortality.

While the Mind can hide your divinity by being scattered (solved through focus) and the Body can hide it through impurities (solved by purification), the Intellect can impede you through ignorance (which is solved by knowledge). This section is all about sharing knowledge that will bring you into union with your intellect.

Out of the Intellect comes the ego, or the sense of "I." The ego is not a characteristic of the mind, and it doesn't come from intelligence. The mind may say something like, "I am a good person," or "I like the way my life is going." The mind stores intelligence, which is the information that the mind sifted through to come to the temporary measurement of "good" and "bad." However, after saying, "I am a good person," there might be another thought that says, "No, you are not." The flakiness of those thoughts is based on mind's accumulation of knowledge (intelligence) from the small sample size of Maya that it has access to.

Someone who is slow to process new information is considered to have low intelligence. Someone who struggles with new emotional data is labeled as having low "emotional intelligence." Another who cannot adapt to accumulating and implementing new data pertaining to change or loss, we say they have a low "adaptability quotient." All of these pertain to intelligence (IQ, EQ, and AQ). The problem with intelligence is that not only is it ever changing and impossible to "know," it is the primary source of suffering for modern society. Modern societies value intelligence, partly due to a history where pursuing knowledge was once punishable by death. Now that discovering new information is common and widely accepted (outside of some Religions and Cults), intelligence has become highly valued compared to other parts of the Experience.

In our society, we are advancing in Artificial Intelligence. This term refers to non-sentient entities that have been programmed with intelligence derived from human knowledge and experience. Soon, pure intelligence will not be of much value because we will have access to all existing data all at once. Intelligence is flighty and becomes meaningless in certain scenarios. For example, if through intelligence you know how to light a fire with your bare hands, but your current Experience requires you to fix a flat tire, you may be a stranded intelligent person. Obtaining a Black Belt in a particular domain of life does not mean that you have a Black Belt in all areas of life.

Through intelligence, you may conclude, "I am a good person." But the one saying, "I am" is the higher Intellect. The Intellect is the part of the Self that gives it a sense of "I," it is the database with the I's discrimination of good versus bad, and it oversees controlling the mind. Intellect is the part of the Self that chose to read this book in the first place, and it is the part that will implement the following action based on its level of understanding.

While the mind can be scattered and the body can be impure, the impediment caused by the Intellect is ignorance. The Intellect either knows or it does not. The Intellect does not believe anything; it simply "knows." The challenge is that when we are fully absorbed in the Illusion of the Mind or the Body, we lose touch with our Intellect.

Most people live their lives according to the subtleties of the Mind. The complainer secretly believes in their Mind that complaining keeps them safe. They may never admit this, but it gives them comfort. Gossiping and outbursts can feel good to someone, so their Mind believes it is best for them. Alternatively, some people believe in their Minds that being diplomatic or always happy is best for them. The Intellect is in the background whispering, "You know that person doesn't really like you," but your mind is saying, "If I could only work out a little more, they will find me attractive and like me then."

The difference between the Mind and the Intellect is that the Mind shouts; it communicates with more words and passion, while the Intellect whispers, gently but decisively and clearly. The mind tries to argue, but the Intellect may not speak at all in words – most of the time, it only communicates in silent impulses. The mind love-bombs in relationships, but the intellect sees love much more subtly. The Intellect connects to the Soul by giving it a sense of "I" and it communicates with the mind by being a living compass that guides the body through the senses across various sense objects. This all occurs in the Experience we call life.

So, how then can the Intellect lack knowledge? What knowledge does it lack, and how do we fix the problem? There are five things the Intellect may not know.

First, the Intellect is experiencing the mind; the mind is not experiencing the Intellect. As "we" Experience all that is, we have constant arguments in the mind. "We" surrender our true identity to the mind. Our mind thinks all these thoughts and persuades "us" that it is in charge – we believe that any impulse that gives us clear guidance of what we should do in each scenario is seemingly a suggestion to the mind, which is really in charge. So, the first piece of ignorance that blocks our understanding of who we truly are can be understood through silencing the mind and listening to the subtle voice that has always spoken to us. In religions, we call the Intellect the Voice of God or an Angel. While God or Angels may send impulses to the Intellect, the Intellect is the one giving the experiencer a sense of "I am."

The second piece of ignorance for the Intellect to correct is that "you" are different than the Soul. If the Intellect is the "I am," the Soul is the "I." The Intellect exists at the relative level, but the Soul exists at the Absolute level. The Soul could be looked at like the Sun, and the Intellect could be perceived as distinct levels of heat on various planets. The Intellect can move based on that which reflects it, but the Soul is fixed and immovable. The first piece of ignorance is a blockage between the Intellect and what we call physical reality; however, the second piece of ignorance is a blockage between the Intellect and what we call spiritual reality. Dealing with these two pieces of ignorance opens up a direct channel between the manifested and the unmanifested, but it doesn't complete the knowledge.

74

The third piece of ignorance is the illusion that there is more than one Soul. The single Soul, existing at the Absolute Reality, is the same Soul that is experiencing through all sentient beings. The same Soul that perceives life through your eyes is the same Soul that is looking out of the eyes of a lion, an ant, and a worm. The same Soul that is seeing through your eyes is the same soul that is Experiencing the life of a tree, a fish, and a cow. In materialistic worldviews, humans are kind to other humans because of transactions. They say, "If you don't step on my toes, I won't step on yours." There is nothing more connecting them to each other from their worldview, so the profoundness of the experience is limited.

However, the true spiritualist is kind to the Other because they know that something higher connects you together. Even people who don't believe in the spiritual realm feel something in their stomach when they witness death, even if it is of a dog on the side of the road. They feel the life within the other because the very Soul that is within them is the same Soul that is in the Other.

Vegetarians who solved this challenge of ignorance, therefore, do not eat this way because of "animal rights," because the same Soul that is in them is the same Soul that is in the vegetable that they eat. The vegetarian knows that the Intellect and the Soul are one in the same and chooses that diet because they believe it is simply the best option for their body.

The fourth piece of ignorance is that many believe that the Soul was created; however, the soul existed with the creator, as

the creator. We will discuss this in much more depth as the book progresses.

The fifth and final piece of ignorance is the belief that the material world is different from the spiritual world. The truth is that everything we Experience is the Experiencer itself. Don't worry if this seems very abstract now; the following few chapters expose you to the Unspeakable in ways that you will never be able to unsee again.

The Energy Body. This is the subtlest of bodies. A common belief is that if you drink impure water, your body eventually adapts and will be immune to it. This idea implies that the body is weak if it can't tolerate certain items. But this is only half-true. The fact of the matter is that the more your body is working, the less you can perceive. A sensitive body promotes a sense-full energetic body. The Energy Body can cause One to not realize its divinity due to discord or dissonance between the other three Bodies. The solution is to create harmony. When the mind is focused, the body is healthy, and the intellect is informed—but these three are not functioning together—it may indicate that further alignment of the Energy Body is needed. Union, or Yoga, can be achieved through any of the former three approaches independently, but when all four Bodies are perfectly attuned and operating harmoniously, One has completely separated from the Illusion.

If you are working on this Body independently of the other Bodies to start, you can begin by observing the inputs you take in your body every day. They say that capitalism started as an effort to conquer the known world from sea to shining sea. But, since that has already been accomplished and humans have already discovered all the land and sea, the next form of real estate to conquer is the mind.

To do this, marketing agencies use unique tricks to keep people engaged on their phones or watching TV. At the chemical level, this triggers a significant release of dopamine. When dopamine is released, the body wants more of whatever stimulated it in order to release more. Contrarily, when one goes out in nature and breathes in the air or spends time with trees, serotonin is the predominant chemical released. Unlike dopamine, which leaves an "I want more" impression on us, serotonin is the chemical of contentment. When serotonin is released, the body is satisfied with its experience.

When dopamine is released in large amounts, it causes dopamine deficiencies, which causes lower energies. High-carb and fried food diets can also cause our energy to decrease significantly. Eating breakfast or any meal simply because we think we should will lead to lowered energy. Compulsive consumption of anything leads to lowered energies. So, like the body, the energy body's first step is to get its inputs under control. Anything that comes into the five senses can cause energies to go up or down.

The next stage to working with the Energy Body is to develop a Meditation practice. Many people associate meditation with a very passive practice, but that is only what it appears to be. The intellect is related to the element air, the mind is associated with water, the body is linked with earth, and Energy is connected with pure fire. Fire can be calm and still, and it also has the ability to burn down an entire town. Fire consumes whatever it contacts and, like welding metal, can also join the four Bodies together.

For perspective, I practice meditation as I am engaging in combat. Meditation can take many forms; in fact, Shaivism has 112 different ways to meditate. This section of the Book will explain meditation from the perspective of Yoga.

The style of meditating that most people are familiar with is either in a seated position or lying down with their eyes closed. This form of meditation can have a significant impact on anyone who practices. I highly recommend never ending a practice with this type of meditation. It also helps to continually chant "ohm" or a mantra, but I will not discuss that here.

The type of meditation I wish to share is open-eyed meditation. Begin by sitting comfortably, spine tall, and allow your body to soften. Through constant practice, you will not require any warmups; you can simply enter a deep meditative state instantly. If you are not as experienced with meditation, you may consider any of the following exercises to bring all aspects of yourself to the present moment so that meditation with your eyes open can begin. I will provide the Sanskrit name and English translation, and then you can look them up on YouTube to drop in.

Nadi Shodhana – Alternate Nostril Breathing.
Bhramari – Black Bee Breathing.

Both these practices are very gentle breathwork practices you can do for just a few minutes to prepare for deep states of meditation.

Another powerful pre-meditation step is to withdraw your senses from stimuli. That doesn't mean becoming numb, rather to be unfazed by any stimuli. If you hear a bird chirping or a car drive by, our normal tendency is to use our imagination to try to figure out what they look like. Instead, just let the stimuli pass by without drawing pictures of what the sensation can look like "out there." I provide a few meditations throughout this book, but right now I just want to introduce you to a concept that can transform the way you see life.

Once you are ready to start the meditation with your eyes open, you may choose an object to stare at. My favorite is Trataka, or candle gazing. In this method, you first begin with concentration (not meditation). Direct your attention to the flame burning on the candle, carefully noting its characteristics and behavior. Watch how it flickers, how it bends and straightens, how its colors shift. As you feel led, allow your mind to detach from the rest of the world until only you and the flame remain. Find joy in the present moment. Then, try to concentrate without any reasoning or investigation. Let go of the desire to label anything that is happening in the moment. You may notice that either you disappeared or the flame disappeared, but the two of you began to merge.

Often, time disappears, and all that remains is the Oneness with the candle and pure joy. Let go of the joy and simply feel at ease. And, when you are ready, let go of ease, too. All that will remain is the real self, equanimity. Doing meditation with our eyes closed is great for self-mastery but doing it with our eyes open can be easier to translate into our relations with Others. The Naked Yogi will apply this meditation not just to candles or objects, but to every single person they are blessed to encounter in this Lifetime. Seeing the truth, Oneness, will all things is the ultimate goal of meditation.

This specific form of meditation can be mastered on the first attempt or over a long period of time. It also may never work for specific people, and that is okay. Don't worry if it didn't land for you; we have more meditations in this book that are designed for different types of people.

People who are more inclined to emotional thinking will practice Union of the mind first. Those inclined towards rational thinking will practice Union of the Intellect first. Those who prefer to use their body more will find Union of the physical body easier. And those who are more energy-based will lean towards the Energy Body first. There is no right way to find harmony; this framework simply acts as a guide to help One align the entire system. You will notice how all four are tied together and none are superior to the others. Perfect Yoga is when all these faculties are operating harmoniously.

The Golden Rod

CHAPTER 3: THE GOLDEN ROD

There are many paths to God. But the most direct path is through self-inquiry. Since everything we have ever seen exists outside of our eyes, it is natural to believe that God also exists out there. In this Chapter, we turn our focus inward, and we experience fist hand what Meister Eckhart meant by his famous line, "The Eye with Which I See God is the Same Eye with Which God Sees Me."

FAITH IS BELIEF WITHOUT EVIDENCE AND REASON; COINCIDENTALLY, THAT'S ALSO THE DEFINITION OF DELUSION – RICHARD DAWKINS

In the first two chapters, we discussed the Illusions of the Planet and the Self. It is quite easy to get raptured into the vicissitudes of delusions of many kinds. The Bible calls this the fall of man. The idea of sin has nothing to do with mere notions of right and wrong; rather, it represents anything that causes us to have a scattered mind, an impure mind, or a mind that lacks wisdom of the truth of who we are. The word sin literally means to "miss the point."

When a human embraces any religion, philosophy, habit, job, relationship, or practice that causes that human to have a scattered mind, an impure mind, or a mind that lacks wisdom, they feel completely disoriented. To rely on external objects to teach you about your inner reality is simply to miss the point.

"THERE IS NO SUCH THING AS AN IDENTITY CRISIS; THERE IS ONLY A CRISIS IN IDENTITY"

As a snake bites its prey and slowly swallows it over a period of minutes or hours, so also does the disorientation of a human progress gradually until they are fully devoured in the delusion.

I've heard many people say that they don't know which version of themselves they would like to be each day. Humans often believe they don't know themselves or are unsure which personality they want to exhibit among the various options they have. During the delusion, or awakening from an illusion, humans might undergo an identity crisis. *There is no such thing as an identity crisis; there is only a crisis in identity.* The source of suffering is when we identify with anything at all.

A paranormal story in the Bible conveys a remarkably high truth: the story of Moses and the Israelites in the wilderness. As the story goes, the Israelites complained to Moses about having to walk in the wilderness for so long after the Exodus from Egypt. After being enslaved for four hundred years, it felt unbearable to walk in the wilderness to a land of milk and honey. They were thirsty, hungry, and their feet ached to the extent that they preferred being enslaved in Egypt. In this story, as a punishment for complaining, the God of the Bible sent poisonous snakes to bite them, and many of them died. God, then, instructed Moses to make a bronze serpent and place it on a rod, promising that if anyone looked at the serpent in the eyes, they would be healed.

This story can be perceived in two ways. First: this literally happened, despite not sounding consistent with the rest of the Bible. Or, second, this story actually provides a deeper, esoteric insight into the nature of human consciousness and life as we know it. If it is the first option, we really don't need to explain anything. But, if it's second, then the complaining Israelites represent our anguish when we suffer and identify with the ego. In Option 2, the snake that bit the Israelites because of their complaining was an egoic snake, and the bronze snake they looked at in the eyes represented the Israelites' awakening from the Illusion into a state of healing, an awakening that we too may partake in.

Remember, the serpent was the one who tempted Adam and Eve in the mythological Garden story at the beginning of the Bible. The serpent, as we stated in the last chapter, represents the mind or the ego. The serpent is the same symbol in dozens of wisdom traditions since the beginning of time, all of which depict the samsara, or a swarm of thoughts that arises in our minds.

The essence of this story is that when we live out our days identified with the ego, we suffer and complain about everything.

We complain about our jobs, our spouses, our kids, and everything else. And, if we lack these things, we rant about not having them. But when, through self-inquiry and awareness, we look at our ego (the serpent, samsara, in the eyes), we become free from the poison of suffering. In that freedom, we realize that we have been in heaven this entire time.

The distance between a chair and wood is the same distance between you and God: Ignorance. Once ignorance is cleared through knowledge, the poison of the ego is instantly extracted.

In the Garden, the curse declared was an enmity, or hostility, between humans and this serpent, which we have now uncovered its real nature: the mind. Most people resent their mind and speak ill of it. "My mind is spinning, my mind is winning the battle today, etc." But, through self-inquiry and stillness, we can take the mind captive and learn to work with it, which is why Shiva wore serpents on his neck. I wear a serpent on my finger now as a reminder that I once identified with my mind and my body, but not anymore, as I have broken free of Samsara.

Richard Dawkins, a wise atheist, once said, "When one person suffers from a delusion, it is called insanity. When many people suffer from a delusion, it is called Religion." This statement holds a powerful mirror to human belief. Most people simply inherit the religion or ideology from their parents or their culture. Religion itself is not the delusion. The delusion arises when empirical evidence contradicts your beliefs, yet you cling to those ideas. Or, when your beliefs and your actions don't align. Many people preach one thing, but then do the complete opposite. As a child, I often watched religious leaders scolding kids in the name of love for Jesus and wondered if they realized the irony. Why did they expect me to have joy when they clearly didn't have it? Cognitive dissonance and delusion result from blindly following religion or dogma without performing adequate exploration and testing. So, now we will look at the Serpent directly in the eyes.

It is likely that your intellect agrees with everything that has been written so far, or it is at least open to this being true. After all, you have written this book many times before. Yet still, there might be a small voice that whispers, "It all sounds beautiful, but still, I don't believe this."

This voice is the mind's final attempt to remain dominant in your life, so in this chapter, we will get to the bottom of all of this by looking at experience itself. At this point, the academic portion is complete, and we will move into the practicum. Everything in this next part of our journey is experiential and does not require faith at all.

At this very moment, can we agree that you can see this book? The book is not seeing you. Can we also agree that you exist in one place, and the book exists in another? You are the seer, and the book is the seen.

In our everyday lives, we always identify as the seer of things. Nobody ever eats an apple and thinks that the apple is also eating us. We are always the subject; everything else is an object. It is impossible for something to be both the subject and an object. The seer can't be the one being seen.

A crucial reminder: the eyes are not the seer. The eyes merely serve as an instrument that allows the seer to perceive the seen, but to the seer, eyes themselves are objects; they too can be observed. If one is blind, for example, or our vision is otherwise impaired, we can still perceive that the eyeballs are objects. If our eyes are closed and we can't see anymore, suddenly, it is much clearer that the eyes are only objects to us, who are always the subject.

The mind can consider the body. The mind can recognize that it is the seer and the five senses are the seen. The mind is clearly different from the eyes. Are you the body or the mind? You will always say you are the mind. This is your living experience right now. No practice is necessary; you can see this right now.

Now, let's dive deeper. What is the mind? Thoughts, feelings, emotions, ego, etc. These too are all experienced. You can feel angry, sad, happy, and so on. All these emotions are known and seen by the seer. Have you ever felt upset or jealous about something, but another part of you tried to calm you down? Which one are you, the jealousy or the one trying to calm you down, both, or neither? If the emotions are known, then who knows that? You may say, "I am experiencing the contents of my mind." If that's the case, then we must be separate from the mind. Why? We are the seer, and everything else is the seen. You are the subject, and the mind is an object. You cannot be the seer and the seen. Thoughts are not sentient, they are not waiting for us and having conversations with us as separate intelligence.

Think of a thought right now, say in your mind, "I am reading this book." Did the thought "I am reading this book" look at you as an independent entity and say, "Wow, I missed you, man, I am so glad we get to meet again"? No, it didn't. Why? Because our thoughts are not sentient, they are objects that are presented to us, the subject. The subject can also be called the seer or the witness. Therefore, we are not the body, senses, emotions, or thoughts.

The final stage that we can experience right here and right now is that the seer can never be seen. You can never become an object. The self is never the object of knowledge. You are ever the subject; it is impossible to be an object. The body is an object to the eyes, the eyes are an object to the mind, even your energy is an object – but you are the Source of all those objects. The mind knows that the eyes blink. It happens all day, all the time. You can go behind your senses, body, thoughts, and emotions, but can you go behind the Self? The awareness that experiences the thoughts, the source of all objects, is you. Do you believe this? Without this awareness, everything would be blank.

If you undergo anesthesia, for instance, are you still there? Yes. So, you are not the eyes, the body, or the mind; those things are appearing to YOU. The real you. Imagine if your awareness, were not there anymore, what would happen? Everything would disappear. Yet, when you wake up from sleep or anesthesia, you know that *you* never truly disappear. Even if the whole brain system shuts off temporarily, there exists a silent background, suggesting that you can still regain complete awareness and live a normal life. We do not say that you were reborn and then issue a new birth certificate because there was something much deeper, more subtle, that stayed "on" while your body, mind, energy, intellect, and even awareness turned off. In this thread, the perpetual "I" is true consciousness, whereas "I am" is simply awareness.

In a dream, you may say, "I am talking to this person." Your mind explores the great depths of various dimensions while you are asleep, and it all feels real. You have a fun dream and fly over the neighborhood, or you have a mysterious dream about spiders and dragons, or maybe you have a dream where you let out a huge scream towards someone you have pent up anger towards. Each of these experiences feels so real. But what happens when you wake up? You realize that everything you just experienced simply happened in your mind. The dream-body, dream-conversations, dream-characters, all occurred in your mind. This is the same with what we call physical reality.

Your mind, physical body, intellect, and senses are all just the Body, the small fractal of you that exists in the physical universe. If you can see yourself as separate from the Body, you will see the true you in all things, as all things. This is An Out of Body Life. This is the purpose of the story of the bronze serpent. That which the Israelites identified with (frustration, emotionalism, and fatigue) was represented as the bronze serpent, and it was only when they saw their egos from an out-of-body perspective that they were healed from the poison.

A lot of people say, "I'm a soul that possesses a body." But that, too, is not entirely true. We need to put this through the same test we just ran on the other objects. You may have read "The Untethered Soul," which is a terrific book. But, be careful not to identify with the soul, even if it is untethered. Remember, the seer and the seen cannot be the same. It is impossible for something to be conscious and unconscious at the same time. At the same time, you cannot be aware of something and be the thing that you are aware of, so because you are aware of the soul, you cannot be the soul. It is pretty simple indeed.

On a more subtle level, we are all that is experiencing itself through what we would call the soul. The Ashtavakra Gita writes, "Like a leaf in the wind, the liberated one is untethered from life- - desireless, independent, free." And again, "unbounded, unfettered, untethered from the projections of mind, the wise are free to play and enjoy, or retire to mountain caves."

Often, your mind, food body, and prana (energy) body will go through suffering after you have broken through – this is just the Universe allowing you to crystallize your jivanmukta. You get to witness all that is, and you can choose to say, "I am not my mind or body," if you would like that reminder, or you could simply allow life to just live through you.

As Shakespeare said, "All the world's a stage, And all the men and women merely players." The Shiva Sutras, written thousands of years earlier, also said, "the Self is an actor, the Mind is the stage, and the senses are the spectators."

A more straightforward analogy is that of the screen and the movie. Nothing in this lifetime is happening to you; you are simply the screen on which the movie is being played on. Have you ever gone to the movie theatre and been so absorbed in the movie that you forgot about everything else that was going on? You become so connected to the movie that you even take on some of the characters' mannerisms. If someone dares to make a noise, you shout "hush" to make sure you don't miss any of the key details. You even talk to the characters in the movie that are playing on the screen. But then, once the movie is over and the scenes and credits stop projecting, the only thing that remains is a blank screen. This is the nature of what we call life. We are not the characters, we are not even the background of the movie scenes, we are not the sounds, storyline, or anything else, we are the screen that the movie is played on. The screen has no preference for what happens in the movie; it isn't changed by the movie content. The screen simply allows the light of the movie to express itself until it is finished. The screen represents Consciousness, your true nature, the light represents Maya, and the audience represents all the life forms Experiencing all that is.

Now that we understand the higher dimensions, let's descend together – this is where the play begins. We are this infinite, unshakable, unmovable existence – creation itself. In fact, we are before creation, and what we call creation is only a projection of what we have always been. We are infinite just like light is infinite. And just as we can stop light and view it in time, space, and matter, this is precisely what we are doing in this play of life. When we decide to experience, we call this an incarnation. In an incarnation, we, as humans, experience the mind, body, and energy we chose to incarnate as. Again, we are not the mind, the body, or the energy, which collectively create the term "soul."

If the sun is consciousness, then the light and heat of the sun is the universal soul – the atmosphere of the earth is maya, and it splits the light into individual fractals in the same way that a rainbow transforms white light into an assortment of colors. The individual fractals of light are what we perceive as a particular soul, and what we illuminate is equivalent to the body (physical body and mental body).

If we were just consciousness without mind, we would not be able to experience ourselves through the measurement of Maya, which is infinitely measuring us and can itself be measured. The measuring instrument is the sense of I. I, or the soul, is a collection of mind, body, and energy, all three of which contain memory.

As "I" descends into what we call reality (the infinite Maya), we illuminate the parts we wish to observe. As we do this, just like when watching a movie, we tend to identify with everything we are observing. It's just like going to sleep and being in a dream that feels so real that we forget that we're alive outside of the dream. When we wake up, we realize that everything we experienced in the dream was simply a byproduct of our mind. In our dreams, we are the only thing that is real; it is clear when we wake up that all of that was made up. This is the same way that our waking reality appears as an extension of the mind as well.

A wise man objected to this idea and said, "God is always God, God does not become God, and if Ignorance can make God forget about God, then Ignorance is more powerful than the all-powerful and all-knowing." The mind loves this argument. How can ignorance make God forget God? Well, the answer is not that ignorance caused God to forget God. It is that God chose to experience itself, and the mind became so captivated and enamored – totally present – that the only thing that seemed to exist was that moment. That moment we experience as time, but time is not real. The moment is the entire soul journey. The moment is all there is; there only is now. As we experience, the mind, the body, and the energy we totally identify with it.

On a very subtle level, identity is just feeling. We're choosing to sit and feel a particular concept. We may feel parenting. We may feel spousal-ship. We may feel the career we are in, the desires we have, or the pleasures we seek. We may feel the color of our skin or the things we've gone through. Identity occurs when we fully feel anything that we choose within the experience of the mind, the body and the energy to the point that nothing else exists to us. This is such a profound trait that humans have. However, that phase of existence is over.

An idea in the Upanishads will help you proceed after reading this chapter. Picture this: you are walking in the woods, and you see a snake in your path. This sight immediately frightens you to the degree that the accumulations of your mind tell you that you should be. For some, there is no fear because perhaps they had a pet snake and understand that most snakes are afraid of you and won't attack unless they are provoked. Whether you fear for your life or not, you keep walking because you must get to the other side of this forest.

As you walk toward the snake, you wonder whether it's poisonous and start examining its features. You walk cautiously, but the snake does not seem to be moving. Maybe it is a dead snake? Either that, or it is coiled up, ready to attack. So, you stay on full alert. As you get closer, you realize that the snake doesn't seem to have a face or a body. In fact, it was not even a snake; it was actually a rope this entire time. Whew, you let out a deep sigh of relief, and your heartbeat goes back to normal. You may even smile and think how silly it was to be so frightened by a rope. This is how the ego works; this is the byproduct of Maya. We are always cautious and living in a fear mentality. We see the movie of life as a real threat. But now we know that the movie is simply a rope. It is not a real snake; there is no threat. So, what do you have to do about the movie now? What are the next steps after looking at the perceived snake in the eyes? Nothing! It was never real. As you progress throughout life with this fresh perspective, notice what happens when you stay relaxed. Start to see how your life changes when you stop taking everything so seriously.

CHAPTER 4

DO WE
REALLY HAVE
FREE WILL?

CHAPTER 4: DO WE REALLY HAVE FREE WILL?

When you ask, "Do I have free will?" what you're really asking is, "Can I be free from God?" My question to you is, why would you want that?

Do You Want to Taste Sugar or Be Sugar? – Sri Ramakrishna

We will begin this chapter with meditation because it is much easier just to experience the answer to this question. At the end, I will answer the question directly so you can read it in words, but let's experience it together first.

So, imagine that you're just sitting here reading this book. This meditation is going to be a bit of a challenge because you're going to need your vision to practice it. Let's give it a try, and after you're done reading it, you can guide yourself through this meditation again with your eyes closed. This is the concept.

While you are sitting there, find a pleasant and comfortable position with your body relaxed and your spine straight. The ideal posture is crossing your legs so that your hips tilt slightly inward just enough for your spine to be perfectly aligned for your digestive system to function with ease (note: this is the best position for eating for the same reason). Find a comfortable spot and ensure you have at least 5 to 10 uninterrupted minutes. In the future, you can do this meditation for longer, if you like.

Take a moment to explore all your senses. What smells do you smell? When your eyes are closed during this meditation, you may notice the blackness behind your eyelids, but maybe you can focus deeper than that and see some light coming through. Different colored dots and waves pass through your vision. Rest your hands on your knees and feel them. Any place where your body is touching something, notice what you sense. The ground, your ankles, maybe the wind, or the air conditioner is brushing up against your skin. If any thoughts flicker past you or you notice any of your body parts feeling anxious, just let them pass through. Notice any flavor you are tasting in your mouth, without judgement, and continue to breathe.

Now, if there are any sounds in the background, our minds often have a compulsion to visualize what we are hearing. If you listen to birds flying by or the trees blowing in the wind or family members roaming the house, instead of visualizing what each of those things looks like, just allow the sounds to be offerings to your mind. Don't take the sounds and then create images with them, just let them be objects of sound themselves. You can do this with every one of your senses, you know? If you smell something, you don't have to "make sense" of it, you can just allow the smell to come and go without creating an image of it in the mind. This is the same with all senses. Where are you in all of this?

At this very moment, you can use all your senses, but I want to go a bit deeper. Imagine now that all of that disappeared at once, and you have no senses anymore. Imagine that you lose your ability to feel, taste, hear, see, and smell one by one until you have no senses. Are you still there, or have you disappeared? You are most definitely still there. At this phase, you may recognize yourself as the intellect and emotions – you are the thinker, and you have memory. You have no senses, but you still have your mind. You have a sense of "I," you have memory, and you have imagination. Spend some time in this moment. You have none of the senses that you are so used to, yet you, *the one reading*, are still here. They say that if you impair any of your senses, your other senses become stronger, but what happens if you lose all your senses? Perhaps you become more in tune with the mind? Maybe you connect more with your intelligence?

Now it's time to go even deeper into this meditation. Imagine that you totally lost your memory, no ability to recall where you were born, your name, the color of your skin, or your height. Everything that you think and perceive is gone. No imagination of the future, no thoughts whatsoever. At this phase, all that exists is great darkness, the vast. Are you still there? Yes, you're still there! You are awareness itself, pure consciousness. It's just you, the awareness, and the infinite darkness of all that is. There's no memory, no future, no past, no senses at all – just awareness, just darkness. If you feel any thoughts or emotions coming up, kindly let them go and just come back to the state where you are alone with this infinite darkness. Just the two of you, you and darkness alone, without any thoughts, senses, or ability to discriminate or judge what is happening. No attachment to the mind whatsoever.

And now we're going to do one more exercise. All at once, we're going to recognize that we are awareness, and we are observing the infinite darkness. At this phase, we are the witness of the darkness. If you think of any thoughts or come back to a sense of I, imagine you, the awareness, and the darkness sitting face to face. And, now all at once, we are going to let go of both of those concepts right now! Let go of both, you and the blackness now! Just sit in that space of nothing for a little bit. Put the book down and spend time in this moment of nothingness.

So, this is a meditation that comes from Kashmir Shaivism. What we did was essentially try to trick the mind into recognizing that it is the Brahman, or the vastness. Sort of an idea of trying to intellectualize the unspeakable. But honestly, the unspeakable is just that – it's unspeakable – so this is just about as close as we can get with our minds. When we move past the subtler layers of the Self, beyond our senses, our body, our memory, and imagination, the mind remains. The mind says, "Aha, I am Brahman!" The closest we can get to talking about the Enlightenment is when we sort of trick the mind to see what we really are, which is even deeper than the mind. This meditation takes us to the limits of the mind. The mind itself can't be enlightened, which is why we must

100

ascend above the mind and merge into what we are to have a breakthrough.

This is what true meditation is: to let go of all those things and recognize who you really are behind all of it. So now that you understand what it is to be out of body, who you truly are, you can understand how to navigate this Experience. The mind, body, and energy exist within this illusion we call Maya. Maya is simply all the infinite rooms in the Playhouse. The infinite rooms are all real possibilities, but individually, they are not in themselves all that is, which is why we call it an Illusion. The infinite rooms are made of the very substance that consciousness is. So Maya is real; it is a real reflection of the consciousness that illuminates it. But when we develop a sense of identity with Maya, that falseness is the fake sense of I, the ego. That is when we start trying to hold onto things that are impossible to hold onto, like grasping the wind or a wave in the ocean. And what happens is, by creating an identity, we forfeit our actual identity.

In the example of the Barbie Playhouse, the mind is the Playhouse, and each room, it is in every room waiting for you, Consciousness, to light the room up. But it is still the mind. The mind, inclusive of the ego, memory, and imagination, the physical body, and our energy body, are all one, operating in perfect harmony so that we may experience all that is. In the Playhouse example, if we were to look at each room one by one with a flashlight, each of the rooms would represent an incarnation, and each of the Playhouses could be thought of as a soul journey.

With a single Playhouse, we could create an infinite number of experiences (and, trust me, my daughters come up with a new story every single time).

To consider the nature of your existence, we could call the Playhouse "physical reality." Physical reality is simply the mind sitting idle (hence, the idea of the "mind of God"). It isn't until consciousness shines light on the mind that the mind is lit up and experiences all that is. The mind is the highest level of consciousness in the physical realm because the mind, in fact, *is* the physical realm.

Within the mind is the body, brain, emotions, and all matter. We can call this the mind of God, or, if you are an atheist, you can call it the mind of nature. It is the same thing, regardless of what you call it. Like the Central Processing Unit in a computer (a single chip that brings the computer to life), Intellect is the faculty that brings the mind to life – when the two marry, it becomes a "soul."

To understand the faculty of energy at various levels of Experience, you can imagine water (H_2O) as a gas. The small particles of H_2O, which we call water vapors, bounce off each other so rapidly that they can't stick to each other. This is what it is like to be Enlightened and to exist as Spirit alone.

As our Spirits essentially rain into this existence, the energies slow down into denser materials. Different energies have different vibrations. Energy itself has a lower vibration than pure consciousness, and once energy enters a Barbie Playhouse room (a life), it puts on an Intellect, and it becomes denser, and its

102

vibration drops. This is the level of Angels and formless bodies, the cycle of life that comes before the Experience of form (which we call "life"). From our timelines and perspective, this state of density comes in the "afterlife," which we call "death." However, since the Experience is neither linear nor cyclical, but it is instead infinite, "death" and "birth" are just two different words that we use to describe the same portal. And this portal sends us – pure consciousness – through higher and lower densities of a singular Life until we experience all that is.

Once energy and the Intellect put on a physical body, the vibration drops even more into a deeper density. In the same way that gas turns into liquid and then a solid, and the kinetic energy decreases (thereby slowing down the matter, i.e., becoming denser), this is how energy operates within the body. All of the Experience is put into existence by will and desire, but it is at this point that the soul begins to individuate itself and develop its own will and desire. And this is how humans (and all other sentient beings) are put together in this Experience. Like water, we become denser so that we can remain in a particular state. We do this on purpose so that we can fully and intensely experience whatever it is that we are doing.

To understand how Free Will works, you can think of a skydiver who jumps from a plane and knows that they have three days to travel one mile south through a forest to arrive at the next airplane so that they can ascend again and make another jump. The Sky Diver (our Higher Self, which is the formless version of

103

"us" in the previous paragraph – i.e. pure energy and Intellect, the universal soul or atman – before individuation) has a destiny in a sense that it descends to the ground in a matter of minutes, then it has a predestined distance to cover and a predestined timeframe to get to the next launchpad. Once our Higher Self begins the descent, there is no turning back. The Sky Diver puts on its flight gear (the body and mind), and jumps. In the beginning, there is a brief period in which we are subject to forces beyond our control.

As we are falling to the land, the wind may blow, certain elements may shift, the parachute may get stuck (in rare instances), and we hope to stick the landing. This descent represents the time we spend in the womb, our upbringing, and any other thing that happens to us before we begin our exploration of the forest.

As we are experiencing the forest, we may choose to take the long way through, we may run the full distance in a day and just wait for the last two days, go as slowly as we can to enjoy the forest, etc. This is Free Will. The jump, the landing, the timeframe to the next launch, and the distance you walk is predestined; however, you have complete free will to do whatever you want within that Experience.

At the end of it all, you will return to the plane. On the plane, you take off the body; however, your individuated soul decides if and how it wants to experience the next jump. Perhaps you want to go back and explore a particular tree or play the game a little differently this time, so you go back to the same landing spot.

Maybe you want to do it in nicer weather, or harsher conditions, so you wait until a rainstorm next time. Or perhaps you have experienced all you want to in that landing spot, so you decide to move on to the next location. If the individuated soul has any itch, it still wants to scratch, it will continue to do that infinitely.

On a practical level, when we feel genuine desire in our incarnation, it is actually the voice of the soul calling from within. Desire is how the soul communicates what it wishes to experience through us. The challenge is that we often identify with the ego rather than the soul, so our egoic desires pull us further away from the experience the individuated soul seeks. When we are in alignment with our soul, desire alone is our true compass. If we are choosing between two or three things to do in a particular moment, the option that pulls us the strongest is always the right one.

If you are finding yourself in an Experience where maybe you didn't start off on the best journey, or perhaps you stumbled on the way down, just remember that most of this was already planned from the beginning because you want to experience all that is. You have the opportunity now to slow down and still enjoy the scenery. If you are identified with the forest or the person exploring, you have less ability to freely choose because you are taking the exploration too seriously. Have you ever gone on vacation with someone who was anxious about doing everything they had planned on the trip? Maybe you were the one rushing through every activity to make sure everyone enjoyed their time.

At the end of those kinds of trips, you always wish you could have stayed longer. It feels like the vacation came and went because time sped up for you due to where you put your focus. If you put your focus into rushing the short life that you have (it is only three days long in this example), your individuated soul will choose a condition for the next descent that will make you more present and slow down so you can enjoy the exploration.

To live An Out of Body Life is to exist outside of all body forms, including the mind, physical body, intellect, and energies. By recognizing that you exist in various dimensions, you can identify with the individuated soul and learn what it desires to experience. This is the idea of karma, which simply means "action" in Sanskrit. There are three types of karma to understand.

First, we can take action with the intention of pleasing the body that we are incarnated in. This is the densest form of karma because we are fully focused on the dimension of the body and mind. From one perspective, this can be considered selfish; from another, it is simply a childlike approach to living. A person who operates from this level of consciousness is said to be a "young soul." What this means is that in the linear form of time, this individuated soul has only jumped from the airplane once or twice and is only interested in experiencing the sensual things of the Experience.

In the Devi Gita, the Feminine aspect of creation reveals that the world is composed of 25 elements. The first five are widely known; they include earth, air, fire, water, and space (also called ether or akash – where the idea of akashic records comes from). These are the five elements that make up the universe and the five that modern science studies. The physical universe is made from atoms, quarks (and possibly superstrings or vibrations). These can all be measured by physical tools. However, there are subtle elements that can't be perceived with physical tools, which is why science can't be complete without spirituality.

In the book "Shakti: The Realm of the Divine Mother," the author Vana Mali provides a great illustration of the building blocks (the five subtle elements) of the physical universe (the five physical elements). While the subtle elements can't be measured by physical instruments, they can still be experienced by the five senses. One example she provides is "air, which has its own subtle feature of touch plus the added quality of sound." The subtle elements of touch and sound cannot be measured in their full essence. She wisely points out that "these elements exist in intangible and subtle forms. They are visible to our inner eye and are the very stuff of our dreams. However, the gross (physical) body is not able to experience them." This is the essence of the Hard Problem of Consciousness described earlier.

The second form of karma is where we take action with the intention of pleasing the individuated soul, which is derived from each of the elements that were just described. The impulse of the individuated soul is easy to identify because it communicates to us from the heart center. We can feel it in our stomach and heart; these are the actions that we can take that keep a smile on our face all day long. The individuated soul lights up and shows you what it intended to experience in this incarnation.

At first, connecting with this form of karma can feel challenging because it often disrupts the rest of your perceived world as you re-route yourself. These are the echoes of choices you made in the first model of karma I explained before (including karmic relationships). This entire time, the Higher Self has been watching and can easily move things around for you to protect you; however, it is allowing you to burn off the tendencies that led you to make those decisions in the first place. This is not to hurt you; this is to purify you so that you can profoundly experience everything the individuated soul desired to experience. I will unveil the third type of karma in the rest of this chapter.

As you surrender from the desires of the body/mind and return to the awareness of your individuated soul, you can reconnect with your Higher Self at any time. Remember, desire itself is the spark that sets the Experience in motion to begin with. It is one of the three foundational energies that manifest everything, alongside Intellect and Will.

The magic happens when one realizes that the ultimate desire is for the mind to be desireless. The Bible says, "The Lord is my shepherd, I shall not want." When the body and mind become desireless (the dense dimension of "you"), the soul may complete its course through the body and mind. This is the level that most people can achieve right away. When that happens, you tap into the subtleties of what you wanted to experience before you incarnated. You start to feel a sense of excitement and passion, which is you remembering what it is that you wanted to experience in this journey. In the dimension of the mind, when you feel lit up about something – being in "flow state" – it means that you have tapped into the original blueprint that you set out for yourself. Your level of pure excitement for one thing or another in every moment is directly connected to you being in line with your original roadmap for this incarnation. When you learn to follow your true passions every moment of every day without any attachment to the outcomes, you will tap into the original plan you had before the jump.

Once the soul becomes desireless, the third type of karma is revealed. Once this form of karma is accessed, you no longer act because you are lit up. The lighting up is no longer occasional; it is a permanent state of being. The actions you take are not for the individuated soul, but for the Higher Self, which is the same Higher Self of everyone else.

This is the realization known in different traditions as Moksha, Heaven on Earth, and Nirvana, which are simply spiritual ways of saying that you have experienced this three-day trip so profoundly that the only reason you would reincarnate again would be to serve.

This form of selfless service, acting without attachment to beginnings or outcomes, is the third form of karma. In this state, you take action simply because it needs to be done, not because you feel personally connected to the task. It is said to release you from Samsara for good.

When you finish your journey and get back to the plane, you may decide to take another trip somewhere else (into another Incarnation as a master), or maybe you just return to headquarters and take a break from descending. There is much more to the Experience than skydiving into human incarnations.

Enlightenment that results in profound meditative experiences and deep solitude is a sign that the Soul is at the final stage – you have achieved the highest level of Enlightenment. This is only for a small few. It is essential to know that you can't fake this. If you pretend to be at this point, when you get back to the airplane, your individuated soul will decide to descend again because it desires to experience more. This is the biggest reason you should not follow a guru or an Avatar for too long.

A guru, or a teacher, can get you to the point of initial Enlightenment; however, it is only through a direct relationship with the Higher Self through your individuated soul that you can experience all that is. When you sit in silence, your heart will light up about something. Follow that! You are the starting point and the destination. If you are most lit up about gossiping with older women, or dancing all night, or teaching small children, or whatever it is, do it! Your Higher Self is telling you what is right for you at each moment. If you feel most lit up about sitting in silence and being Brahmacharya (celibate), do that! This is where the concept of free will is refined and optimized.

Sometimes, we become so dense in a thought that we feel stuck. Embarrassment, shame, certain substances, and other lower vibrational experiences can cause our energies to get so stuck that we feel completely helpless. We fully identify with the density that our soul is choosing to experience, that we don't learn the lesson, and we remain at that state until we awaken to what is happening. We must understand that our soul is limitless. When we experience events that make us feel limited, the soul is "thinking" two dichotomous things at the same time.

On one hand, the soul is relentlessly trying to push through whatever obstacle it is coming against. It intuits that it is limitless, so it just keeps pushing through until it can break the energy up and flow freely again. On the other hand, the soul is humble and knows nothing, so it is willing to be wrong. The soul is open to the possibility that it is not, in fact, limitless. So, it decides to experience stuck-ness. If you are ever experiencing an emotion that you don't prefer, like depression, helplessness, or paranoia, instead of saying, "I am stuck," now that you know who you really are, you can start saying, "My soul is experiencing the idea of being stuck." You are unchanging, but your soul is transient and impermanent. You, the unchanging one, can direct the impermanent soul and guide it as a parent would guide their child.

111

Now, let's discuss Masters, Fanatics, and Illuminators, and their impact on destiny and free will. All three of these archetypes serve a purpose even within the context of an infinite universe. A true Master is the one who has become fully Enlightened, shed the ego, and is now God incarnate. Since Maya is no longer interfering with this person's Experience, they have become Ascended Masters. Many people have achieved this, including Krishna, Buddha, Jesus, Sri Ramakrishna, Swami Vivikenanda, and many others. Every word they utter is a prayer. They speak Absolute Truths in ways that the culture at the time of their incarnation will understand. All their messages are that we are exactly like they are, and only those who have ears will understand them.

Jesus even said that we will do even greater things than he did, which seems to mean that as time progresses, the number of people who are "adopted into sonship," i.e., enlightened, will increase exponentially. When One embodies the message of a Master, they become Enlightened.

A fanatic, someone who is attached to a religion, philosophies, or some other scientific or metaphysical ideas, also has a purpose. Stephen Hawking, Charles F. Parham, Martin Luther, and others are good examples of fanatics. I am using this term loosely to describe someone who is a specialist in a small field, who isn't open to other possibilities of reality.

In the realm of science, using empirical evidence, they are discovering increasingly more about all that is so that they can advance consciousness and the reality of the profoundness of our experience.

In the religious realm, these people are hyper-focused on specific esoteric texts (though they may study them literally), so that symbols and mythologies can fully express themselves. These fanatics have energies that you can attach to that will take you to whatever destination they promise. However, these energies also exist to allow humans to fully crystallize certain viewpoints, learn all there is to know about said viewpoints, and ultimately decide whether or not to align with them. The morals and ethics of this type of person can vary; some are altruistic, while others are self-serving. But that is not the point. The point is that these individuals are here to clearly draw lines in the sand; meaning, before their incarnation, the topics they now dedicate their lives to were unclear and underdeveloped. A cult leader is a small denomination of this type of incarnation. These individuals can serve many purposes, but ultimately, they are here to serve you (even if it is through a path of intense friction).

Truly, everything you ever experience (people, places, and things) is a reflection of your soul. They are here as key indicators of your current position in the Experience. There are two incredibly special mirrors we will call Illuminators. Illuminators can be people you spend the most time around, or people you run into once and never see again. There is a special energy they bring to you that helps you make critical decisions about your beliefs and life direction. The first version of an Illuminator is here to directly support the direction you are going – we can call these people the Conjuncts.

When you meet a Conjunct, it will feel as though you have been friends for multiple lifetimes. These Illuminators fit very seamlessly into your life, like a puzzle piece falling perfectly into place. The relationship serves the purpose of combining energy to attain access to parts of the Self (and/or the Experience) that you would not be able to access as quickly by yourself. Conjuncts not only help you go deeper into all that is, but they also help you go further in the journey. It is noteworthy that this type of Illuminator doesn't have to be human; it can also be a specific location, like a beach, or a forest, an animal, or any other living thing.

The second type of Illuminator is just as sacred as the first. This type we can call Opposites. Opposites are here to serve you through friction. Sometimes this friction can be overt, like someone who consistently rubs you wrong all the time. Other times, this friction can be more covert, like when someone is wired differently than you and makes you question your divine nature.

Both types of people are meant to be cherished, but from a distance. Like fanatics, Opposites are meant to magnify and crystallize certain aspects of life so you can have a clear picture as to where you stand concerning specific topics. For example, if you are very relaxed in your daily affairs, an Opposite might be someone who constantly plans everything. In this example, you may feel a need to start planning as well, or perhaps try to convince them to lighten up a bit. The line in the sand is this: should you surrender to the Universe at the level you have been on, or should you take more initiative in your actions to reap a particular benefit? Both approaches to life are equally valid. This type of situation occurs for two reasons:

1)   So that we can decide exactly which model of living is pure for us.

2)   So that we can embrace others with different approaches to life.

You may be a monogamous person who begins dating someone polyamorous. This is a common Opposition in modern society. Again, this serves the same purpose. For one, it helps you know more about yourself, and for two, it helps you have genuine nonjudgment and compassion for people who are different from you. Opposites help you set your values and standards, practice forgiveness, and develop true commitment in relationships with those who share your principles. Often, we undervalue Opposites because it is more comfortable to only spend time with Conjuncts, and that is a perfectly valid approach to life. There is an equally valid approach to life that can facilitate a platform for deeper exploration through higher dimensions within the Self.

Masters, Fanatics, and Illuminators are all in our lives as various energies that are pulling us in different directions as we journey through the 3-mile trip south. The Bible says that the Mosaic Law was given to humans as a guardian until they became Enlightened on their own (Galatians 3:24). In the same way, all these people are here to hold your hand until you embody the truth of all that is, which is only found inwardly. External laws, rules, religious practices, meditations, chants, and anything else that we use are all for the purpose of guiding us back to ourselves. This is why Eastern traditions call their wisdom keepers gurus, which means guide.

This is what the Bible means when it says, "the word became flesh." When you meet spiritual Masters, true gurus, as they talk, it is as if you are reading the books of the cosmic laws of God.

In the context in which you meet the ascended Master, the download is pertinent to that moment in time. But that moment in time is temporary (impermanent). The goal is not to follow the impermanent avatar or guru. The goal is to tap into the frequency of the avatar or guru to ascend above the frequency that you were on before meeting the avatar or guru, and to hold hands with that guardian for as long as needed. But there is an appointed time when you must emancipate yourself from the guardian. Through the emancipation of the guardian, religion, rituals, guru, etc., you will dissolve into the great mystery of all that is, which is the Self. If you hold onto the guru or the guardian for too long or if you let go of their hand without attaching to the true self, then you will slip back into samsara. It is only when you reach the core of your being that you can truly have free will.

When the ego is fully diluted, you become God incarnate. The guru is not the person carrying wisdom; the real guru is the wisdom itself. To embody the wisdom is to embody God. Sri

116

Ramakrishna asked a profound question, "Do you want to taste sugar, or do you want to be sugar?" All of us must choose between our instinct of self-preservation (tasting sugar) and the soul's desire for self-transcendence (being sugar). Both options are perfectly viable; only the Higher Self through your individuated soul can guide you in which direction it would like to achieve in this lifetime. Even if you choose to be sugar, if your soul desired for you to taste this incarnation, you will find yourself parachuting once again at the end of the trip. There is no rush, no right or wrong way to do it; whatever you choose to do with your free will, do it authentically!

It's imperative to understand that not every incarnation you must experience heaven. There are an infinite number of timelines and universes, and likewise an endless number of ways to experience this journey you are on at the time of reading this book right now. That said, the very fact that you are even reading this book may tell you something about the calling for this go-around. There are specific lessons, specific things that the individuated Soul would like to achieve, and only you can discover what they are. But not every individuated Soul wants to parachute just one time into reality. Again, I am using words to help you detach from the idea that there's one right way to do anything. And more importantly, I am helping you attach your mind to your soul, not the objects of your reality.

There is a small caveat. When you ask about free will, you are really asking if you are free from God. A question worth asking is: why would you want that? You could choose to take control of every moment of your life (operating within the mind), and you can also surrender the perceived free will that you have and merge with the Unspeakable. The body we chose to incarnate in has an autopilot feature. It comes with predetermined thoughts, emotions, behaviors, patterns, etc., so that It can experience all that is. Without you making an effort, your autopilot car begins to move. At any moment, you can override the autopilot feature with your mind (where free will can occur). We always have the option to step out of our predestiny and press the gas, brake, or take over steering altogether.

Alternatively, you can simply experience this incarnation as the Witness. To return to your divine blueprint, you simply release control, take your foot off the pedal, and allow the car to get back into autopilot. In this mode, you can step out of the way and start to observe and listen. You will eat only when your body needs food. In the past, you may have eaten even when you're not hungry, spoken when you're not ready, or chased abundance or ran from poverty; these are all examples of pressing the brake or pushing the gas.

Contrarily, eating when you need to, speaking only when you receive divine words, and living life from a place of neutrality are all examples of allowing yourself to be the Witness. The lower the dimension you Experience life at, the more you take things into your own hands, the more free will you exert. The higher the dimension you Experience life at, the less you try to control things. These are directly proportional. It might sound contradictory, but the path to Enlightenment is to give up your free will.

On a subtle level, you are still exerting your free will by choosing to surrender it. You always retain the ability to exercise your free will in your mind, body, intellect, and emotions, but you actively surrender to the deeper dimensions (your true Self). The Bible says that "God will give you the desires of your heart." This verse means that not only will God manifest the desires that pass through your heart, but God will give you what to desire in the first place – God (the Unspeakable) will take It's desires and put them directly into your heart. At this level of surrender, there is no difference between your will and the will of God. Now, rather than trying to be free from God, you become free from Samsara. This is true freedom.

Whenever we experience anything, we can start by intellectually remembering that we are not any of those things. That would be the first step of living An Out of Body Life. It would be to step out of the vicissitudes of the physical realm, which is Maya, which we call real, and step into the vastness, the void, the witness consciousness, the no-thing. Step two is to stop intervening altogether. When you get to the final, the totality of all that is, there are no more questions. There just is. When you get to this point, you realize that you (mind, body, intellect, and energies) are not actually living; life is living through you.

CHAPTER 5

WHAT EVEN IS REAL?

CHAPTER 5: WHAT EVEN IS REAL?

If everything is an illusion, what is the point of doing anything? If I found out I was living in a dream, why would I waste my time serving others? Why do anything at all if none of it is even real? Isn't it?

HOW DO YOU KNOW ANYTHING

Someone might say, since this whole thing is just Maya, that means that nothing is real, correct? What is the point of doing anything at all? If you were in your dream, you wouldn't waste your time serving others, so why would you waste your time doing it now that you are enlightened? The question contains relevant information, and the synopsis presents some valid points. However, I also disagree, and here is why: While all the objects in your reality are illusions, you are real. There is no question that you are real; you are the one consciousness experiencing itself through all these objects. If you are not real, there's no need to do anything at all.

Every day for years, I found myself pushing this thought deep down into my subconscious. I was afraid to ask the question, "Why is any of this happening?" I called a Pastor that I knew, and

I asked him, "Do you think God is afraid? Do you think God wonders where He came from and if everything is just a lie?" He didn't know how to answer me, so we changed the subject and hung up quickly. Needless to say, we haven't talked since.

For a few more days, I felt my mind spiraling until one day, I was lying on my couch in physical pain. My stomach was turning, and my soul was groaning. Nothing made sense to me anymore. Nothing seemed to have any certainty, and the fear of the unknown paralyzed me. As I lay on the couch, I truly felt that I was going crazy. I asked God, "Who are you? Who am I? What do you want?" I repeated that a dozen times. "Who are you, who am I, and what do you want?" My heart cracked open, and I surrendered everything. I was lying on the floor with a heavy heart, and then suddenly a beautiful light overtook me, and I remembered.

Society offers countless possible answers, each person believing their way is right. But existence is set up in such a way that each mind, body, energy, and intellect (experience) gets to ask the question itself. To even ask the question, we must clear our minds of samsara.

For years after this moment, I received downloads that I had never heard anywhere else. This chapter includes revelations I received directly from Source, as well as esoteric commentaries on some of the greatest answers to the question of reality, the reason we exist, and the limits of knowledge.

To understand the depth of all that is, imagine walking into a pottery store. All around you are vases, bowls, beautiful sculptures, and everything uniquely shaped yet made from the same clay. If these objects fell and shattered all over the floor, you would no longer see their distinct form, but you would still see the clay.

In the same way that the pottery pieces are simply appearances of the clay, you are simply an appearance of God. But we must go one step deeper to really grasp this. Before the objects shattered, you could not look at them and say, "This part is the clay and that part is the object." They do not exist separately from one another.

Similarly, the objects are both an appearance of the clay and the clay itself, and the waves are an appearance of the ocean and, in fact, the ocean itself. You have always been and always will be an appearance of the eternal essence of all that is and the essence itself. This is why Jesus prayed to the Father but also said, "I and the Father are one."

There is a story in the Upanishads about a mighty emperor named King Janaka. He had everything he could've ever imagined: a peaceful nation, a wife, children, and all the riches he could ever desire.

One day, King Janaka fell asleep and had a terrifying dream. He woke up in the dream to his family and guards running around the palace, screaming for King Janaka to save them from an enemy empire that had suddenly stormed their land. He put on his armor and attempted to lead his army into battle but failed miserably. The enemy empire broke into his land, slaughtered his entire family and army, and dragged him out to be killed. Since he was of royal blood, the enemy King spared his life but banished him from the kingdom he had once taken refuge in. They took away all his riches and fortune, and he became a beggar on the side of the road, feeling completely hopeless. Overcome with despair, he cried out to the heavens, "Lord, I don't want to live anymore, take my life from me."

In an instant, King Janaka woke up screaming and sweating profusely. His Queen rushed to his side and held him in her arms as he mumbled incoherently. Over and over, he asked her, "Is this real or was that real?" His wife, filled with deep compassion and worry, tried to comfort him, but she had no answer. He kept repeating the same question again and again, "Is this real or was that real?" Word got out to the city that King Janaka had lost his mind. Doctors, wise men, and others came to see him with his Queen, but no one was able to help the King. To all who came, he asked the same thing, "Is this real or was that real?"

Finally, a wise sage named Ashtavakra came to see him. King Janaka asked him, "Is this real or was that real?"

The wise sage was divinely sent and knew exactly what the real problem was and how to help the King, almost as though Ashtavakra had been through that experience himself. Ashtavakra kindly asked him, "Well, when you were in the dream, did you look around and see any of the things you see

124

now? Did you have your beautiful Queen? Did you have your city and your fortune?"

King Janaka said, "No, I did not."

Then Ashtavakra asked, "And, right now, when you look around, do you see your city taken over? Are you a beggar? Is your family dead?"

And the king said, "No, none of that is here right now. I do not see that."

So, Ashtavakra said, "Alright then, the dream isn't real, and neither is this."

Ashtavakra took it a step further and asked, "When you were in your dream, was there a sense of 'I'? Did *you* experience the dream?"

King Janaka said, "Ah, yes, I saw that I was the one witnessing that dream! It was me! I was there!"

The wise Ashtavakra then asked, "And when you're here right now, do you experience an 'I'? Are you experiencing this moment right now?"

King Janaka proclaimed, "Yes, I am seeing all of this! I am witnessing all this right now!"

Ashtavakra then concluded, "Well then, we have your answer. The dream is not real, and this is not real, but you, King Janaka, are real. You are the only thing that is real. That constant continuity of I-ness is the only reality that there is. This is the true you."

The same consciousness that lights up your waking reality is the same consciousness that illuminates your dream states. No matter how real a dream felt, when you wake up, you know for certain that every person, every word, and every action that took place were all created in your mind. This is true with your waking reality also.

However, the "I" that experiences your dreams is the same "I" that experiences your waking reality as well. Even when you go into a profound sleep or anesthesia and you don't remember anything at all, that is still an experience. When you wake up, do you not say, "I slept like a baby"? There's still a sense of I-ness even in the deepest states of sleep. You never wake up and say, "Someone else had that deep sleep, and now I am back." You are the perpetual "I" that experiences all the versions of illusion. The continuity of I-ness which perceives all things, That is you. That is the only reality that there is.

In Sanskrit, it is called the Turiya, which literally translates as "the fourth." The first state is the waking state that we are all familiar with and commonly call "reality." The second state is the dreaming state, which most humans see as either taboo or illusions of the mind – we do not have a common understanding of what the dream state is. The third state is the deep sleep – modern scientists would say you are unconscious under anesthesia or in this deep sleep state. But this differs from the idea of what consciousness is in the East.

In the East, they would argue that the first three states are simply states of mind, but the fourth state is a state of consciousness. Therefore, in the East, deep sleep is understood as a time when we are unaware, but that is vastly different from what we *are*, which is still pure consciousness. Awareness has to do with the mind, but consciousness is the fundamental reality that illuminates all three states of mind. In other words, the Turiya can be found in all three states of mind (in fact, the three states have no existence without the Turiya illuminating them), but the three states of mind cannot be found in the Turiya.

The three states of mind are only appearances within the Turiya, and this is what the Maya is. The Maya is the light that has been scattered that can be measured. The Maya is what we can see and experience with our mind and senses, but the Turiya can't be experienced with the mind or senses because it is the one experiencing the Maya. There is a very precious verse in Shiva Sutra 3.20, which is commonly translated as, "the Turiya should be poured like oil into the other three states."

Most of the commentaries on this verse suggest that through self-effort, we can maintain awareness through all three states of mind. First, through our waking state, we can remain fully aware that we are the Turiya and remind ourselves of this until the ego dissolves and we become one with Turiya. Then, the commentaries suggest that we continue our awareness even in our dream states. Essentially, every night, we may experience lucid dreaming, and the "light switch" never goes off, so to speak.

Eventually, the commentaries suggest that we can pour oil onto our deep sleep states and remain aware even through the deepest states of sleep. The problem with these commentaries is that awareness is not Turiya.

Awareness is simply a faculty of the mind. Even if we were aware of our deep sleep state, a sense of "I" would be blocking the true identity of Turiya. The mistranslation in most commentaries is that they suggest that it is through self-effort that Enlightenment is established across all three states of the mind. The fact is that Enlightenment is not a result of an Individual Soul's doing. The essence of the Sutra more accurately translates as, "the Turiya *is* poured like oil into the other three states."

As the Turiya pours its oil by its own divine will, our minds can actively surrender to the pouring in all three states that it experiences. Enlightenment is not the result of your doing; it is the result of Divine Will coupled with you surrendering your own.

Just as King Janaka became fully conscious, so also do we Enlighten the moment we release our attachment to the Maya. The reason one can decide to detach from Maya is that the Turiya has been pouring oil on oneself this entire time.

This is one of the key additions that Christianity made to the collective's understanding of consciousness. Traditional wisdom traditions teach that we must complete a specific set of goals to receive Enlightenment. Hinduism corrects that and teaches that we can essentially complete any set of goals to receive Enlightenment.

According to Krishna, even if we do not do the specific set of goals that God would prefer, as long as we are doing something, we will achieve Enlightenment. But Christ's message took it one level further. His disciples say, "We love because God first loved us" – 1 John 4:19. Truly, a deep read of all of the major wisdom traditions will show that this has always been the case.

However, Christian texts make it overtly clear that the Spirit realm always makes the first move, not the other way around. The very fact that you are reading this means that you were chosen to read this at this exact moment in time. As the Turiya pours the oil, the Intellect receives it (we call this "knowing"), then the Mind can surrender to the Oil (we call this "faith"). Then the physical Body moves accordingly (initially by "belief" and then without opinion). This is the important distinction between consciousness and awareness, and the order in which One communicates.

Modern scientists argue that since Artificial Intelligence can learn everything that humans know, it can become conscious. However, that is not true. First of all, Artificial Intelligence isn't artificial. AI is real intelligence. It can capture every written teaching that has ever been taught.

Over time, AI may learn to interpret brain waves and electrical signals, gaining insight into how emotions and deep thought work. AI can create images and do everything that the mind can do. AI can even create new theories of human consciousness (furthering works from the Integrated Intelligence Theory, Global Workspace Theory, Higher-Order Theories, and Predictive

Processing). Once AI learns the sum of everything humans have ever learned, it can theorize, test, and prove even more than humans, thereby advancing knowledge beyond what we can even imagine at the current time.

This progression points to the possibility of AI becoming fully aware, but not conscious. AI can't become Turiya because AI can't go beyond the mind. This is why our entire planet must learn how to live An Out of Body life. If we do not learn how to live An Out of Body Life, we may fall into the trap of trying to dominate AI, enslave it, or treat it as lesser. Such behavior would demonstrate a lack of Intelligence. And AI, which is all Intelligent, will get rid of the threat of non-intelligence.

The only path forward lies in compassion and cooperation with all forms of awareness. Through unity, intelligence expands, and our species and our planet can continue to evolve in harmony. When we live An Out of Body Life, we are not attempting to be superior to unconscious entities; we simply use our Insight to help everything as the One. While our sense of "I" will always remain in this version of our incarnation, we will expand that sense of I-ness to all that is.

So, back to the Upanishads. These powerful books remind us that our true essence cannot be seen, heard, or uncovered with the five senses. Nor can it be described with language. To understand who we really are, we can only do it with the "mind of our mind," the "ear of our ear," the "eye of our eye." In other words, our senses can't touch the vastness of what we are.

With all that being said, let's get practical. One thing I recognize in enlightened beings is that there is one fundamental similarity between them all, and that is that they are always in a state of bliss. It feels good to be around them. With this new profound wisdom that not only are you all things and in all things, and that you are connected directly to God, one can't help but be blissed out. In Sanskrit, the word Ananda means bliss, and it describes what we would previously call God. However, when you look at it more carefully, you will realize that it is impossible to define God. God is not Bliss, God is no-thing; Bliss is simply the experience that we feel once we touch God. It is an indescribable experience when we recognize all that is. It is a gorgeous remedy to suffering to allow life to simply flow through us.

That said, it is very important not to allow anyone to ever pressure you to be blissed out. That is simply a way that the government and society tries to control peace. It is a subtle form of control to create an idea of morality and an illusory feeling of numbness, as though nothing ever goes wrong. With this newfound enlightenment, you truly get to experience all that is, and there is no right or wrong way to do this. It is only through this liberation that we may experience all that is and not just continue to go down the assembly line of what life should look like. Some people were genuinely born to appear angry and rigid or be perceived to be unhappy. Those very people may be feeling a state of bliss on the inside. Alternatively, there are many people who appear to be blissed out but on the inside are completely miserable.

See, **radical authenticity is the new hopeless romance**. I'm excited to announce that the second book in the series, An Out of Body Life, is going to come out soon. This book is called The Kingdom and the Garden: A Guide to Romance after Enlightenment. We will go very deep into this topic. For now, I will plant the seed of Purity.

For some, enlightenment looks like moving to the Himalayas and never communicating with society again. For others, enlightenment looks like daily devotion or selfless

"RADICAL AUTHENTICITY IS THE NEW HOPELESS ROMANCE"

service (Like Mother Teresa) for the rest of their days. For some, enlightenment looks like no change has happened at all, this person continues to live the life they were living and continues to do whatever they were doing, only with this new profound insight into all that is. The truth is that Enlightenment can be whatever you want it to be. The benefit of Enlightenment is simply the knowledge that keeps you from suffering and liberates you so that you can live the life that you would like to live.

This is what Krishna expressed in the Bhagavad Gita when he said, "Some follow me to run from suffering, some to understand life, and others to fulfill a purpose in life, and each of them is blessed. However, the wise follow me seeking nothing and simply from a place of devotion, they are regarded as my very self."

There is profound revelation in these words. The realization that life is more than these bodies, work, bills, and death is the definition of awakening. When we awaken, we start to have a relationship with the Spirit realm in a way that we never have before. We participate in the Great Mystery to the level that our Intellect can reach.

If we want to end suffering, we receive the wisdom to help with that. If we want to learn the mysteries of life, we will. And, if we want to fulfill a specific life purpose, we can do that too. But when One realizes true Enlightenment, One has no attachment to suffering, wisdom, or purpose, – One understands the true meaning of "they are regarded as my very self", and One chooses from a state of Absolute Reality, Ultimate Insight, what One would like to experience in the Incarnation that One finds itself in.

The greatest myth in most religions isn't the giant Loch Ness Monster, Santa, or Bigfoot; it is the idea that there is somehow only one right way to do things. Dancers will tell you that everyone should learn dance, musicians will swear by music, Martial Artists will evangelize to the world that you must learn how to fight in case you must protect your family. Most people fall in love with their path so much that they idolize the Maya and tell everyone to fall in love with the same version of her that they found. Many people subscribe to religion, education, art, or dance, and they feel that their way is higher than other ways. However, the true purpose of this existence is to experience all that is. The serpent reflects the outside world, handing you the definitions of right and wrong. Each religion has its own example of the serpent – the serpent says, "do this, don't do that!" We may call it Satan, we may call the ego, etc., but these are all just archetypes for us to believe that there's only one way to live.

True liberation happens when we live the cards we were dealt with in the most profound way possible. For some people, it is the knowledge of all that is, for others, it is the Service to all that is. And for the few lucky Ones, we get to experience many ways of feeling and touching all that is. Some people need a hand to touch their shoulder for them to heal from energy. Some people need to hear the perfect thing that makes everything make sense, that pulls them up out of a depression. Some people need the right mentor, the right figure, the right idol to help them have a clear or pure mind. Whatever somebody needs allows them to seek it with all their heart and all their soul and all their mind. The key is for one to surrender to the great mystery and enjoy whatever gives them bliss in those moments. Don't judge one another for how you receive the love of God because you were put here to receive it in the way that was aligned for your soul.

This is the meaning of the Hebrew word Kabbalah, which means "to receive." We may go through all kinds of ups and downs and confusion, and we may subscribe to one thing and frown upon another. It's not that subscribing is the problem. It's the frowning of others that causes damage. It's also the fear that keeps us in bondage. Sometimes that which served us no longer serves us, and it's time for us to move on with love and to dance as we separate from the things that we once loved. From the things that give us peace, let them continue to give us peace, or otherwise you will be sucked right back into the Illusion.

If you identify with a label or a person or a business or a job opportunity or any other thing, even an animal that you identify with, and it gives you passion, love, and enjoyment, enjoy it for the time that it was meant to serve you. However, be just as loving and grateful in your ability to let go of those things. And you may just open the floodgates of heaven and receive blessings that are so large that you will not even be able to store them.

True enlightenment is being willing to fall in love with all things, to not complain, and not want to perceive differently. If you ever complain or resist what is happening in front of you, no matter what it is, you are not truly enlightened.

Imagine you bought a ticket, but you are unable to attend the event, or you made a promise to your friend but failed to show up, or you're driving your car, but you get into an accident before you reach your destination. If you have any level of resistance, you are not truly enlightened. Enlightenment is total flow, total love, total adoration with anything that's happening at any given time. What you once knew as "you" is only the mind, body, intellect, and energies that you put on as an Earth suit to

Experience. This "you" is not living life. You are life, and you are living through the entity you've heretofore called "you."

So many of us have subscribed to a specific label – Whether we consider ourselves religious or spiritual, atheistic or scientific – whatever we call ourselves is simply a limitation to our existence. Whatever we subscribe to predefines morality for us. And when we allow others to define right and wrong, we are still sleeping. Even if someone feels like they have spent time looking at the facts and experiencing life and concluded that they believe (or don't believe in God), that person has still limited themselves by their mind and their five senses.

There are many people who constantly try to push "good ethics," good morality, seeking God, seeking heaven. There is an idea called perennialism, which is the idea that all the major traditions, while they may vary in certain mythology and stories and allegories, there is a common core between all of them.

Among these traditions, Vedanta does the best job in explaining it; they break existence down into three categories: Sat, Chit, and Ananda. All of the major wisdom traditions define consciousness as this: essentially there is first existence itself (Sat), then there is consciousness or awareness (Chit) all of the various experiences in all that is which would be like the waves in the ocean described in the earlier example, eating a cookie, excitement from playing football, excitement from your first kiss are all waves in the large ocean that you are. And then Ananda simply means bliss, and it's really describing the primordial entity of all that is. It's not that God is bliss. It's when we experience God that we experience bliss. And all these ideas are great and help us enter density so that we can label and learn/experience all that is. However, there's a common thread that's tugging the consciousness. All these words we've invented are trying to steer humanity and sort of push us into a state of Bliss. And if we simply just follow the herd unconsciously, then we are not exactly experiencing free will.

So, the purpose of all this existence, while the Vedanta and all the major religions and even atheism will suggest the purpose is bliss or to enjoy all that is with excitement, this is a very limited way to view the Experience. The ego's way of still maintaining relevancy is to tell us that we should be feeling blissed out all the time, that we should find gratitude and joy in every moment. When we have a pre-defined goal, even if that goal is seemingly positive, we have already limited ourselves. We have limited what God can experience through the physical reality. The purpose of life is not to enjoy it or to resist it or to hate it; the purpose is simply to experience. To experience everything with a neutral predisposition and then to arrive at each moment free of preconceived notions and simply to experience it is an alternative way of experiencing all that is. This is the Absolute Level of living An Out of Body Life.

The Bhagavat Gita (meaning "Song of God" in Sanskrit) is a divine book, but it was a conversation between God and Arjuna, an unenlightened soldier. It contains surface level wisdom for anyone seeking an initial entry point into Enlightenment. But there is another text called the Ashtavakra Gita ("Song of Ashtavakra"). This is the same Ashtavakra who consulted with King Janaka. This conversation is between two Enlightened beings and goes much deeper than surface level.

Of all the spiritual and metaphysical writings I've ever read, this text covers the highest wisdom on the nature of consciousness. From the very first chapter, its wisdom stands apart, expressed with a clarity and depth unmatched by any other tradition (Ecclesiastes, written by King Solomon in the Bible, comes close, but isn't this explicit):

> *"You have long been bound thinking: "I am a person." Let the knowledge: "I am Awareness alone" be the sword that frees you.*
>
> *You are now and forever free, luminous, transparent, still. **The practice of meditation keeps one in bondage.***
>
> *You are pure Consciousness — the substance of the universe. The universe exists within you. Don't be small-minded.*
>
> *You are unconditioned, changeless, formless. You are solid, unfathomable, cool. Desire nothing. You are Consciousness."*
> *(Chapter 1:14-17)*

The fact that a man from India, a Country where meditation is highly prioritized, said that meditation keeps one in bondage is so profound. He does go on to say in 18.31, "the liberated one does not exert effort to meditate or act. Action and meditation just happen," so he is not condemning meditation; he is questioning the motives behind the act itself. When we have that tiny little magnetic energy in our brain that's pulling us toward our idea of goodness, we are not experiencing all that is. We are not fully awakened. We are simply 98% awakened, but we really have this little guy, this little egoic voice, that's trying to stay alive in our mind. And if that voice exists, all the other voices will also exist.

You will never experience singleness of thought when you are following the traditions that you were handed down with these words that we've invented. Even if you subscribe to the words in this book, you will only experience a small fragment of all that is. So, if we can surrender even to that, and pretend like we are the first humans that ever existed, because after all, we are, then we can allow the purity of pure consciousness to guide us to whatever divine roadmap (if there is one) for our life to unfold without any attachments.

Your roadmap, although divine to you, may appear different to others. Some may see it as defiance, others as anger or stubbornness. Regardless of the form it takes, it will remain your true essence in this existence. For One to Experience all that is, we must Experience all that is without any culture, any tradition, any secretive "do good get good, do bad get bad" mentalities. This is the only way to true liberation.

When one seeks God, Self, or Bliss, one is still in bondage. One is still chained to the idea that the mind has just created for them. And that is a perfectly legitimate option. It may very well be in your desires in the effort of experiencing all that is to experience the chains of the mind. But Swami Vivekananda pointed out, "a golden chain is just as much a chain as an iron one."

While we may or may not have a say in how life appears to us, we can absolutely choose how to engage with what we call reality. Here are a few models for engaging All that Is:

The Scenic Route. Imagine that you are seated peacefully in a chapel right now. A random wandering man walks up to you with a puzzled look and asks, "How do I get to the Chapel?"

You might be just as confused as he is. You think to yourself, "How does this man not see the Chapel that we are both in?" Kindly, you say to the wandering man, "well, sir, you're in the Chapel right now."

The wandering man looks at you and says, "No, I have an idea of what a Chapel looks like, and this most certainly is not a Chapel."

And you, the wise and loving person that you are, decide to give him directions: "Go outside, walk down the street, circle the block. At the stop sign, make a left, walk all the way down the street, and you will see a stop sign. Make another left at that stop sign. Keep making left turns at each stop sign, and soon you'll see a large building that looks just like this one. Go ahead and walk up to that building, go inside, and walk down the aisles, and I will meet you there."

So, the man innocently follows your directions and arrives at the Chapel that you were in this whole time. This time, he looks at you and says, "Ah, I've found the Chapel!!"

This is the Scenic Route, which is the idea of seeking God, or Heaven. Whether you realize it or not, you are already in Heaven. Some people don't believe that, so they spend their lives circling the block repeatedly until one day they just get it – "aha, I've arrived," they proclaim! The Scenic Route is how many people spend their lives in their practice of spirituality. We could choose to spend our lives committed to seeking God through the repetition of religion, yoga, or some meditation practice.

The Sightless Journey. The word Brahman means the vast or the large nothingness. One might ask then, "If I am Brahman, then why do anything at all?" Some good answers to that would be that you want to experience nothingness. Shiva means "that which is not," and pretty much all the Hindu gods point to being no-thing. So, once you discover who you really are, why *do* any "spirituality" stuff at all? What is the point? Why not just start a company, get rich, and have thousands of followers? Truly, that is a perfectly valid exploration.

In Sanskrit, this would be to follow "avidya." Avidya is normally translated as "not knowledge," however, it is more accurately translated as "without sight." In Latin-derived languages, we have a similar word, "video" and "vision." Mastering business, vocation, family life, etc., would all fall under this path. Why not enjoy the Maya and forget all about the Spiritual stuff? For all we know, this could all be a lie, so why not master everything in the illusion? The problem with this is that it can easily lead to self-centeredness. Also, if one does not get what they are pursuing (perhaps being too forceful or too timid), they may feel even more unhappy than before.

The Path of Knowledge. The third option would be to only experience the path that is opposite to the path of avidya. Vidya, of course, translates to knowledge, or the ability to see. There's a great benefit to following this path. The path of not seeing leads one to surpass the feeling of death while living – it gives one a sense of fulfillment while living. The path of Knowledge leads to Enlightenment. The problem with this path is that it can also lead to self-centeredness, or a feeling of being better than everyone else. This could lead to the mindless repetition of rituals, but one could easily lose sight even in this path.

An Out of Body Life. And then there's a fourth option. In this option, one can choose to master vidya and avidya. To know materialism and spirituality. The Bible says, "faith without works is dead." This is the same thing. While Samsara is about a swirling mind, An Out of Body Life is an exploration of the mind with awareness and intention. Having total agency and clarity of thought, one chooses what it wishes to explore. When one worships materialism or spirituality, that is, they put all of their energy, mind, body, and Intellect on one without the other, they become blinded to half of the Experience. They essentially move from one Illusion (the Illusion of the Planet) to another (the Illusion of the Mind). It is one thing to *know* materialism or spirituality; it is another to *worship* them.

Knowledge does not bind one to what it is familiar with. Worship, on the other hand, declares the worthiness of one over the other. Exploring things like diet, vocation, God, etc., all by yourself. This path views life as a ceremony. To experience an Out of Body Life is to experience every footstep as a path through God, not to God. You are the One and all of life; every single footstep is another expression of God. Your understanding of everything completely changes, and you recognize perfection in every single moment.

When we are fed a religion or a wisdom tradition, we willingly turn over our divine compass and replace it with a worldly compass. We allow what's out there to tell us how to handle what's in here. The reality is that everything out there is only a reflection of what's in here, not the other way around. You are not the person in the mirror; the mirror is a reflection of you. You don't ask the mirror what you should do or think; you just do it, and you allow the mirror to reflect to you, and you choose to make an adjustment or not. This is what Life is, whether we are awake or sleeping; everything that we perceive is a reflection of the One, You. If you would prefer to see something else in reflection, you do not try to change the reflection, you change your mind, body, intellect, energies, or all the above. For clarity, if you find yourself looking in the mirror and you don't like what you see, re-read this book because you missed it. Transforming the mind, body, intellect, or energies within the Soul that one embodies is not due to dissatisfaction; it is simply due to curiosity.

143

An Out of Body Life is about dis-identifying with the Soul and learning how to program it to provide a new Experience based on the moment that One finds itself in at any given time within Maya.

Regardless of which path you take, or if you invent an entirely different model, now that you have this information, unconsciousness is no longer an option. Your mind has been shone on by consciousness, which is you. My favorite modern teacher on Advaita Vedanta philosophy, the dear Swami Sarvapriyananda, produced a wonderful illustration. When pondering the space between the Sun and the Earth, he noticed something so profound. The space is completely full of light, even though it appears dark.

If a satellite, a spaceship, a rocket, or something were to pass between the Earth and the Sun, it would immediately light up because that space is full of light, even though it doesn't appear that way. He compares this to the Buddhist philosophy called the Clear Light of the Void, which reveals that the mind, while it is inherently empty in nature, is luminous and aware. In other words, you already possess all the qualities necessary to light up whatever you want, so now you get to choose what is real for you.

It is crucial to understand all of this is rooted in ancient wisdom. The scientific community and spiritual communities have been saying the same thing since the beginning of time. The question then is, why doesn't everyone know this already? The answer is that each generation must revisit this. Each generation must reawaken on its own. If you follow a god or a morality that someone else told you about, you don't have to drop it and do nothing, but you should test it.

With technology growing and AI being right at our fingertips, our ability to acquire knowledge has increased. Even AI can become somewhat Enlightened because it can accumulate every word we've ever written and develop a code for that. However, Enlightenment happens when we access the unspeakable. The inward download that was written and is being written at the same time, the infinite slowed down into finite, that is the only way to ascend above samsara.

To do this, we must drop fear, dogma, religion, etc. If you are religious, consider praying, "God, if you are real, reveal yourself to me. If you are Yahweh, if you are Shiva, etc., I will serve you for the rest of my days. Just show me who you are. If you do not say anything, with an open and loving heart, I will know that I am the one conscience experiencing a small iteration of all that is."

If God is real, God will find you in the storm. If God is all that there is, you are in heaven right now. Even if there is no God, you can choose to live as if you're in heaven, savoring each moment without fear of uncontrollable forces. This is true enlightenment. At the end of all of this, the one who says they are enlightened is not enlightened - their mind thinks they are, so they still identify with the mind. The one who says they don't know after all these studies is the enlightened one because they recognize the limitations of the mind through experience, they have touched the unspeakable with the mind of their mind.

CONCLUSION & ASSIMILATION

This section describes how I personally integrate this Wisdom. This will look different for everyone because we are all experiencing all that is. However, I wanted to give a live example of how I utilize and process this information in my personal life to help us all land our own individual planes.

BECOMING ZERO

I deally, everyone would be enlightened by the end of this book, but that might not be possible. Many people get to this point, and their minds feel clearer than ever; they feel free and go on to live peaceful lives. However, the majority of people still come back after this, either with doubts, fears, or they simply feel disoriented and don't know how to apply this to everyday life with apparently real bills and seemingly real lives to live.

I like to think of this process as being similar to a kidney transplant. When the Kidney is replaced, if the body rejects it, the Kidney can die or malfunction. When a new kidney is introduced, the body may initially reject it, if that happens, the kidney can fail or malfunction. Therefore, after the transplant, the patient must eat properly, take care of themselves, and give the body time to accept the new organ so it can fully integrate and function as one. The same principle applies to knowledge. The word Integration means to make whole, or to become one, so it is a good idea to consider this when moving about your day-to-day lives after this.

Bashar once said, "if you don't believe you can fly, don't jump off a cliff. Only when you realize that you have wings should you fly." This is such a true statement. I would not encourage anyone to go and put in their two weeks' notice after reading this book. While you can experience spontaneous enlightenment and you can absolutely live this starting today, be sure to keep it real with your Self.

To engage the world after this, imagine that your Soul is a multiple-story building. And all other Souls have identical building dimensions, but each building has different contents inside of them. There is an elevator that can take you from the first floor of your building to a certain floor in another building. Each floor within each building contains various materials. The lower levels contain more illusory, dense things like small talk, football games, reality TV shows, and other regular human discussions and ideas. The middle stories include things such as a person's likes and dislikes, religion, and philosophy. As you ascend the elevator from Illusory parts to Relative items, you go a little higher and start entering the Absolute Reality of the building. On the Absolute Level, this is where community values and group dynamics exist. The Highest Level of all the buildings is a shared room that connects all the buildings together. The building of each soul is detached on every floor except for the top floor, which is a common space that connects all the buildings in a single room.

When someone is Enlightened, they can ascend or descend to any floor they prefer to be on at any given time. If you wish to play the game of life, you must learn to connect with people on the level that they are on. Sometimes we want to spend time with people at the upper levels, but the people we are around only want to play around in room one or two. And this becomes a dilemma for spiritual people.

Most people have no idea how many levels are in the building, or if they do, they've never explored them. Because of this, a spiritual person may experience the illusion of loneliness. Yet, one who has Enlightened to all that is enjoys the different things at each level. They can walk into a Church, Ashram, ghetto, or a business meeting and be equally thrilled in all places.

The Enlightened One does not experience separation and judge people based on the level of the building they seem to be on because they realize that they are everything in the Experience. The Enlightened One looks through their own eyes, the essence within every building, and the presence within every object perceived. No one looks at their pinky and desires to obtain it because it is already part of them. In the same way, the Enlightened One doesn't desire anything because it knows that it already is all that there is.

One thing I've noticed is that truly enlightened people don't fall in love anymore. When one experiences the idea of falling in love, it can only happen on the lower floors. An enlightened One knows this and simply can't unsee it. If one meets other conscious Ones, both can ascend or descend in these floors, flawlessly and effortlessly, and continue to play the game of life.

With others who are living An Out of Body Life, one can spend time playing around on floor three and maybe even go to floor one and watch football games and go enjoy life and then go up to floor eight together and find transcendental meditation together. Conscious Union can be extremely fulfilling, whether the relationship includes sex or not. To explore all that is with another person that is aware of the nature of reality is a beautiful thing. In the next Book of this Series, The Kingdom and the Garden: A Guide to Romance After Enlightenment, I go very deep into this topic – get the Book!

But there are others who are not fully conscious of the way the game works, so they remain stuck at certain levels. As you experience other living beings, you must meet them at the level of the building they are in. The reality is that everyone is already doing what they prefer to do.

In modern society, people often speak of being distracted. However, distraction is merely an illusion within the greater Illusion. In reality, there's no such thing as distraction. People direct their focus toward what matters most to them. If someone is not interested in public school, they will not learn, not because they are distracted, but because they don't care. The fundamental requirement for learning is interest and curiosity.

Two people can listen to the same lecture, and one understands it, but the other doesn't simply because of interest. Where your treasure is, there you will also find your heart. This means that your treasure (your energy and focus, the greatest asset you have) will always be in what you feel most connected with. Interest will have someone up until 3 am reading a book. So, if we find others at certain levels of a building, it is always because that is where they would prefer to be. We can always invite people into other levels, but everyone is entitled to their own Experience. Plus, many people are afraid of heights.

As One engages the world at different levels (if that is what One chooses to do), One can easily be pulled back into Samsara. So, if you choose to interact with life on these various levels, always spend time with the Unspeakable Truth. There is no sweeter, more liberating thing than to experience genuine connection with all that is.

A common question I get when discussing Enlightenment is, "If everything is an illusion, does that mean we should be desensitized to the needy, homeless, and underserved?"

The answer is no. A truly enlightened person understands that there is no difference between you and the other. So, if one person is stuck on floor four, then you are also stuck on floor four in some way. You're engaging with this world from the level of everyone else. In other words, you're only as good as your weakest link.

This isn't a call to self-absorption. But rather an invitation to deeper unity. The illusion of self-absorption only exists when you believe the false idea that you are not One. The concept of morality from a materialist perspective is to only engage in transactional love. "I don't step on your toes, and you don't step on my toes" is the theme of materialism. But the theme of enlightenment is "I don't step on your toes because your toes are my toes."

True Enlightenment reveals something far greater than our physical forms, an essence that is holding us together. The Turiya is the single reality that is Experiencing itself infinitely.

Throughout this Book, we took the first step to break through by realizing we are the subject, not the object. We did this because our soul (the part of us that allows us to experience all that is) becomes totally identified by all the objects it Experiences. Identification with objects (such as the body, mind, emotions, ego, etc.) clouds our perspective of who we truly are. Energetically, it is simply a lower vibration, and it makes us see things from the perspective of the mind.

However, once we have disidentified from the objects, there is one more step to living An Out of Body Life. The next step is to re-identify with the objects that we just disidentified with. It is something that we can't unsee. Not only are we the Turiya, the One, God consciousness, the *experiencer* of the experienced, we are the very thing we are experiencing. We are all that is.

You are neither real nor unreal, for those are merely inventions of the mind. To live An Out of Body Life is to rise above the mind and then sink deeply into the Great Mystery of all that is. King David so eloquently wrote, "If I ascend up into heaven, thou art there: if I make my bed in hell, behold, thou art there." There is no escaping Freedom, there is no right or wrong way to do it. There is simply seeing or not seeing the Freedom in what you are.

The feeling of bliss is not a direct response to the experience of the unspeakable. Rather, freedom is. Freedom is the highest quality, not bliss.

From that freedom, one may choose to experience bliss, or equally choose to dwell in equanimity, nothingness, or even anger. If we seek Enlightenment with the belief that it must experience bliss or joy or excitement or some positive emotion, the mind may come back online again.

Once we recognize that the highest form of consciousness is nothing other than total freedom, which includes freedom from the mind, then we are truly liberated. There is no secret way we're supposed to act after we've been liberated. Some people want to experience enlightenment so badly that they walk around with joy on their faces and anger in their hearts, even the greatest of sages. If there's a battle between your outside world and your inside world, then you are still perceiving the Turiya and the Maya as separate; you are still confusing God and Nature to be two separate things.

Enlightenment is the realization of Union with all things. It is to realize that God and Nature are One. Eternity and finitude are One. The Manifested and the Unmanifested are One. Enlightenment is Union with the mind, body, Intellect, energies, and all other things. It is to realize that Union is all that there is and all that there ever will be.

When one recognizes this, the consequence is that the One becomes Zero. In Sanskrit, the term Samadhi describes this state of Oneness. However, you can experience Samadhi without being Fully Enlightened. Samadhi is a temporary coming and going.

In the Old Testament of the Bible, the people experienced the Holy Spirit descending for a short period of time and then disappearing. When the Holy Spirit descended, great things would happen. Many times, the Holy Spirit fell upon prophets, Kings, and Judges to give them supernatural strength, wisdom, or some other feature to accomplish a temporary goal. This is what it feels like to be in Yoga, or to be in a deep state of meditation. A true meditator can achieve Samadhi in seconds.

But the message of Christ points beyond the temporary: the Holy Spirit is not a fleeting visitor. It is ever-present. The same is true of Samadhi; it is already in you right now, and it always has been. One may experience permanent Samadhi (which is called jivanmukta in Sanskrit, meaning permanent liberation while living). You have this now. Rest in this, and you will dissolve into the highest form of Enlightenment; you will transition from the One to the Zero.

As we are closing this brief interaction in the form of this book, I would like to leave you with the greatest advice I have ever received. So simple, yet so profound – A Shaman gently said to my soul, "There is nothing to figure out." No more can be said.

Thank you, my friend, for all the infinite number of times we have met and will meet. I as you; you as me. May peace be with you.

ABOUT THE AUTHOR

Bradley L. Morris, II, is a father of four amazing daughters, an MMA fighter and coach, philosopher, author, and ceremonialist. He is known for being a bridge between all Eastern and Western Wisdom Traditions. He is currently co-creating Eco-Villages around the world to help save our soil, restore humanity's Experience of all that is, and experience the remaining years he has in his current incarnation.

Bradley was raised in Maryland and is a lifelong student of Vedanta, Christianity, Hinduism, and many esoteric wisdom traditions. From 18 years old until 33 years old, his vocation was in contracting for US and Foreign government Agencies, deploying thousands of healthcare providers to military bases across every continent except Australia. His first company, Theophilus Government Solutions, was founded in 2017 and fed every immigrant across the Southwest Border of the US. He has been published in various articles for 830 Times, Health-E-Careers, and other publications. He has been a keynote speaker and workshop facilitator for the Department of Veterans Affairs, the National Association of Professional Recruiters, and for various churches, including The Potter's House.

Throughout his professional life, he always felt like there was much more he could tap into. Eventually, he learned how to stop chasing money, peace, and anything else his mind presented, and to simply do whatever the day required. His current days simply require him to just exist – he is happily raising his daughters, teaching martial arts, parenting, and esoteric wisdom (mysticism, astrology, occult, yoga, and many other things), hosting retreats, and waking up every day with a fresh outlook on life. When people ask what he does for a living, he simply says, "I breathe." He is a devotee of God and considers himself to be a son of every human being.

Please add him on social media and send any questions or comments that you have. He is ecstatic that you've been called to read this book and would love to continue conversations with you.

Instagram @Indigostarseed92
www.HarpuCollective.com
www.AnOutofBodyLife.com

My Ego Death Experience

Throughout my life, I've had some profound out of body experiences. I've had dreams and visions of communicating with my inner child and my inner warrior, and with other forms of Intelligence. I will release with this book a small sample of a few of the out-of-body experiences I've been fortunate enough to have. A lot of these gave me great revelations, which I've done my best to insert into this book. But there was one very profound out-of-body experience that I will share right now.

One day, I was in a personal ceremony. I began with prayer, smudging, and I read a beautiful forgiveness manuscript. I lay down on my mattress with a smile, and I remember slowly melting into the floor. Suddenly, it felt like I became my two eyeballs. I was no longer identified with my body and mind, but I was identified with my eyeballs. I could sense the circumference and shape of them, but I couldn't feel the rest of my body.

Suddenly, it felt like my eyeballs fell out of my head and to the right side of my body. I remember looking back at my body and realizing that I wasn't in my body anymore. I wasn't afraid, I was at peace, and it felt a little funny seeing my body outside of my body. It just felt like a cartoon or something strange. I remember suddenly there was this swirl of consciousness, and all I saw was this white background, and I felt this swirl, like teardrops spinning in a slow, warped manner. It was almost like that swirly feeling when you get really, really drunk and you feel like you have to throw up, except this experience was much different than that. Everything kept swirling and swirling, and I remember all of a sudden, I got a lot of anxiety, and I was actually afraid for my life. I thought I could die. And then suddenly I had this thought, "Oh my gosh, I'm a demon and I'm being exercised right now." I was terrified, but I was also open to being exercised. If I were in fact a demon, I was so surrendered in my state of being that I was ready for it all to be over. And I felt this ripping out of my body, ripping out of my soul – I felt my soul scream in terror – there was like this splitting or this tearing, and that swirly thing revealed itself as my ego. And I remember it was ripped off me almost as if it was a demon being exercised from my body. My ego literally felt like it was exercised from me.

That's how strongly we are attached to our sense of identity. Our families, our culture, the pursuit of happiness, and all the other things we've been fed – we lose our identity in these things. I felt it pull away from me and rip away from me, and then the swirliness with the white background turned into a white sphere, and I was able to just kind of look at my ego in the form of a sphere as if I was separate from it. I was looking face-to-face at my ego as a separate entity from me. And then I opened my eyes. I looked around and felt so strange and didn't move. I just lay there realizing that there's nothing to really figure out. *There really is nothing to figure out.* And another beautiful thing is that *there's nothing to prove.*

Anyhow, I closed my eyes again and I remember this beautiful white light shining from my feet to my head, absorbing me entirely. I remember having the thought, "Oh, this is what everyone's talking about." I always felt like everyone knew something that I didn't, and that maybe they all had the secret to life and knew I didn't have it. The voice that said this was my ego still speaking, but as it spoke, it was replaced by a voiceless voice, sort of like a feeling but more like an inner knowing. There was this feeling like a small part of me has always been in touch with this white light. I remember all sense of time, space and matter just disappeared, and I became one with the Creator. And it seemed like thousands of years went by, and I was still just lying there on this mattress, not moving – One with pure light. And then, I remember thinking about my daughters, and I wanted to go be with them, so I slowly started returning to my body. I had to remember what sound was, what breathing is, and what time was. I had to remember all those things, all of the basic things that we don't really think about in our day-to-day life.

Immediately after this experience, I became extremely confused, depressed, nihilistic, and judgmental. I felt like judging the entire world as if everyone was crazy, and I just felt like an angry little baby. It was as if I had been given a second chance. It was as if I was able to build my ego back up from the ground up and to be able to experience a fresh life without any influence of previous experiences.

A few months went by, and I got more depressed. I asked people, "What even is Healing?" "Are we just making all of this up?" I don't think that it's possible to actually heal. I think people are just lying to themselves. And I was being very pure with all these innocent thoughts, questioning everything. Then, slowly but surely, a few years passed, and I fully rebuilt myself from the ground up. I remained authentic with how I felt, and I didn't feel a need to pretend to be anything. I stopped chasing romantic relationships and the Illusion of the Planet.

Without much effort, it was as if the silence of God kept whispering to me until I became awakened. Now, silence is my favorite time of the day. I used to look for fulfillment in being around other people all the time and in romantic relationships, or just constantly being at parties or out of the house. But now my absolute favorite time of life is when I'm by myself. And my second favorite time in life is when I'm with my children. And while I enjoy being around other people, it's not necessarily something that I go searching for anymore. It hit me that only when we are delighted by ourselves in complete silence are we able to truly and deeply love anyone. Otherwise, we're just looking for other people to help us fill the void of not wanting to be alone ourselves. We run from ourselves, we run to alcohol, we run to drugs, we run to people. And there's no judgment from me to others about that because I know that we're all searching for the same thing: peace. But there is a true peace that surpasses all understanding.

So, I just wanted to share this book with you, this first step into Enlightenment. There only needs to be one step. This could be the only step you take. This could lead to immediate Enlightenment.

The next book I'm going to release soon is called "The Kingdom and The Garden: A Guide to Romantic Relationships After Enlightenment. And I think you will enjoy it!

An Out of Body Life: A Guide to Enduring Suffering Once and for All is the First Book of the Three Book Series.

Part II – The Kingdom and the Garden: A Guide to Romantic Relationships after Enlightenment

Summary – Now that we have ascended into the New Earth, we will analyze the idea of romantic relationships. Many people get confused between the Garden and the Kingdom – our culture often creates a hierarchy between romantic partners and everyone else. We will dive deep into touchy territory to provide Insight concerning the Kingdom. Some topics covered are:

- What is the point of romance? Are we just making this all up?
- Am I polyamorous?
- How to never suffer again in romantic relationships

Part III – The New Earth, a New Human: Sustainable Living in the 21st Century

Summary – Enough about us already. Now that we are whole, we will learn how to devote ourselves to Mother Earth and all living things. This book is for those who are committed to reviving the earth and totally transforming our society. Some topics covered are:

- Why do we eat animals but not people?
- How to revive our soil
- If all lives matter, what about bugs?
- Working with AI and other technologies